THE MERIWETHER LEWIS MYSTERY

WESTMINSTER PRESS books by *Wilma Pitchford Hays*

REBEL PILGRIM:
A Biography of Governor William Bradford
THE MERIWETHER LEWIS MYSTERY

THE MERIWETHER LEWIS MYSTERY

by WILMA PITCHFORD HAYS

THE WESTMINSTER PRESS
Philadelphia

COPYRIGHT © MCMLXXI WILMA PITCHFORD HAYS

All rights reserved—no part of this book may be reproduced in any form without permission in writing from the publisher, except by a reviewer who wishes to quote brief passages in connection with a review in magazine or newspaper.

ISBN 0–664–32493–2

LIBRARY OF CONGRESS CATALOG CARD No. 70–141194

CREDITS

American Philosophical Society: 91
Four Winds Travel, Inc.: 29, 38, 47, 53, 60, 64, 66, 70, 75
Missouri Historical Society: 103
Tennessee Conservation Department: 114, 117, 120, 122

PUBLISHED BY THE WESTMINSTER PRESS®
PHILADELPHIA, PENNSYLVANIA

PRINTED IN THE UNITED STATES OF AMERICA

*To my father's family
who were early settlers in
Upper Louisiana Territory*

Jefferson had a grand dream:
An America wide and free from sea to sea.
Lewis made the dream come true!

Contents

1
Man with a Dream

YOUNG MERIWETHER LEWIS stood beside one of the twin chimneys that formed each end of his house, Locust Hill. He showed a workman where to repair loose bricks.

"And while you have fresh mortar mixed," he said, "mend the rim of the well at the stables."

He glanced down the long green slope of land edged with pear trees. The fruit was ripe and should be harvested. He must prune the trees that were hardest hit by last week's wind storm.

The sun came through the early morning fog and touched with brightness the tops of the Blue Ridge Mountains west of him. Meriwether paused a moment on his way into the house for breakfast. What a beautiful country his great-grandparents had chosen when they came from their homes in Wales and England. Both sides of his family, the Meriwethers and the Lewises, were first settlers in central Virginia. Even now his neighbors, living on plantations and farms over the forested hills and rivers as far as he could see, were his uncles and cousins.

Meriwether entered the house. His brothers and sisters were still asleep, but his mother was downstairs. She placed a platter of ham and eggs on the table, then sat down across from him.

"I rode over to check the corn on that new parcel of land in Clark County," he said. "The storm left the corn a little sorry-looking, but the ears have set on well. We'll have a crop."

Lucy Meriwether Lewis Marks nodded. She had the good sense not to talk while he was plainly planning the day's work on the plantation. But her blue eyes showed her deep affection for her eighteen-year-old son, who carried the responsibility for their large family.

Meriwether Lewis had been five years old when his father, Captain William Lewis, died of pneumonia while a soldier in the Revolutionary War. His mother, left with three small children, had married again, a friend of Thomas Jefferson, Captain John Marks.

After the end of the war, Captain Marks moved his family to the land he claimed on the Broad River in Georgia. Although Meriwether Lewis had inherited his father's estate at Locust Hill, he was too young to manage it. He had moved to Georgia with his mother and stepfather and family while his uncles managed Locust Hill for him.

Shortly after he was thirteen he had returned to Locust Hill and taken over the management of his estate, with advice from his uncles. At the same time he attended a small school with neighborhood children, taught by Parson Maury. Later he studied with several well-educated men in the area to prepare himself to enter the College of William and Mary at Williamsburg.

But when Meriwether Lewis was seventeen, his stepfather died. The young man invited his mother, his own sister and brother, and the Marks children, his half brother and half sister, to Locust Hill to live with him. He drove to Georgia with a team of horses and a large carriage and brought back his family.

Now Lucy Marks smiled as her son finished his ham and eggs. "I'm glad the corn crop looks good," she said. "We'll need it to feed the men and families working on the plantation. You've managed Locust Hill well, Meriwether. Your father would be proud of you."

He stood up. He knew how fortunate he was to have such a mother. People said he looked like her, slender, medium height, dark-haired. He was like her in other ways too.

Although she had pretty dresses and could dance with the best at a party, she wasn't afraid of hard work and responsibility. She could use a gun if she chanced upon game to feed her family. She knew how to treat the illnesses of her children and servants with herbs grown in her garden or found in the woods and fields. She was a wonderful cook. Even Thomas Jefferson, now Secretary of State for President Washington, bought smoked hams of her.

"I'm going to ride to Monticello," he said. "I want to see how the peach grafts are doing, those I helped Mr. Jefferson do in the spring. I'll try grafts on our own orchard if his are successful."

At Monticello, Meriwether gave his horse to a stable boy and walked through the garden toward the orchard, where he knew Mr. Jefferson could be found almost any pleasant morning. Past dogwood, laurel, crab apple, and poplar, he found his older friend. Tall, his red hair streaked with gray, Jefferson was inspecting a leaf of some flowering shrub he had brought back from France when he had represented the United States there.

"Good morning, Lewis," the older man said. "What do you make of this whitish insect scale? Not exactly like any I've seen before."

Lewis bent over the shrub. "Looks somewhat like that on the lilac," he said. "I should pick off the infected branches and burn them. Only way I can control insect scale."

Jefferson gave him a quick look, not altogether pleased. He prided himself on his knowledge of gardening and had not expected immediate recognition of a pest about which he had been in doubt.

"How are the peach grafts doing?" Meriwether Lewis asked.

"Growing," Jefferson said. "I've just looked at them. Come with me to see how the weeping willow twigs are sprouting, the ones I brought from Philadelphia."

As they walked along the path, young Lewis knew that something was bothering the older man. When they stopped before the weeping willow twigs planted near a pond, Jefferson scarcely glanced at them.

"They will make a beautiful sight someday, reflected in the water," Lewis said.

"Yes," Jefferson agreed. Then abruptly he changed the subject. "Don't think I'm short with you, Lewis. I read something in the newspaper last night that disturbs me greatly. You know how long I have hoped that an American would first cross the continent? that an American would first find a way over the western mountains to the Pacific Ocean, so the United States could claim, by right of exploration, the vast unknown territory beyond the Mississippi and Missouri Rivers?"

Actually Lewis had heard little about Jefferson's hope of an American being first to cross the continent, but he was immediately fired by the adventure and patriotism of the idea.

"Has someone agreed to go?" he asked.

"Someone *has gone,*" Jefferson said, walking back and forth on the path. "Britain's Alexander Mackenzie has reached the Pacific. After the attempts I've sponsored so quietly, the British are ahead of us. Do you know what that could mean?"

"No," Lewis admitted.

"The few states we own right now, along the Atlantic Coast, could be all of the United States there ever is to be. The Mississippi River would be our western boundary. If the several different parts of this continent are owned by England, France, and Spain, we could always be at war over something, as Europe is today. This new America will have no place to grow."

At once Lewis saw the danger. "Now that Mackenzie has reached the Pacific, does the Far West belong to Great Britain?" he asked.

"Not quite that bad," Jefferson answered, "because the Scot crossed the continent too far north to affect the western territories I want for the United States. We want to explore the Missouri River, and what lies west of it. The Missouri would make a broad water highway inland, farther than any white man has ever gone. I've tried several times to send men west by different routes. All of them have failed. How I wish we had a man who could explore the Missouri and on to the Pacific before the British do it!"

"I'd like to be that man," Meriwether Lewis said.

He was almost as surprised to hear his offer as Jefferson was.

The older man shook his head. "You have Locust Hill to manage and your family to take care of."

"Locust Hill is in excellent shape, sir," Lewis pleaded. "Now that my mother is home, she could manage easily. Uncle Charles would advise her."

The urgency of Jefferson's dream to gain the far west for America was so great that he seemed to hope, for a moment, that this young man might carry out his plan.

He said, "Lucy Marks couldn't have better counsel than your uncle Charles. Everyone respects his judgment and listens to him."

"I'll tell her at once," Lewis said.

Jefferson shook his head. "It must be someone I can trust, and I can surely trust you. But you are much too young to carry out such a grand and dangerous plan."

"I'm not afraid," Lewis urged.

He would not brag, but he hoped his older friend remembered that he had hunted alone in the wilderness since he was eight years old. Food had been scarce during the last years of the war. His family had needed meat. Raccoons and possums were hunted best at night. Many times he had gone into the dark forest alone, except for his hunting dog, and brought back wild game.

Jefferson smiled. "I know your courage," he said, "and your good judgment too. Captain Marks used to say that you were not only a good shot, you kept your head in an emergency. That's another trait a leader must have, to be able to think in the face of trouble."

"Then?" Lewis asked hopefully.

"You are too young," Thomas Jefferson said regretfully, "to lead successfully the kind of expedition I have in mind. The man must have experience in dealing with other people, particularly the native Indians. You've never even talked to a red man, have you?"

Lewis shook his head. He had seen Indians passing through the forest when he was hunting. As a boy he had hidden from Indians who were on the warpath in Georgia.

"Very little is known of the tribes in the West," Jefferson said. "I am told they are fierce and warlike. My dream, of an America that stretches from sea to sea, can come true only if the Western Indians accept us. The man who explores the West must persuade the Indians that we are their friends."

"I wouldn't want to ruin your plan," Lewis said, "or undertake something for which I was not prepared. I hope you find the right man before the British do."

He was still thinking of Jefferson's dream of gaining the entire west for America as he rode his bay horse across the fields to Locust Hill. If only he were ready to lead such an exploration! It wasn't only the adventure he craved. He wanted to gain the new territory for his country.

His mother had told him that his father was one of the first to volunteer in the Revolutionary War. William Lewis had marched with the militia into Williamsburg to seize Lord Dunmore after Dunmore had confiscated the powder supply of Virginia. His father had served during the war without pay, saying he loved and defended his country from loyalty, as he would love and defend his own family.

Meriwether Lewis prized his father's coat of arms, which hung in Locust Hill, with its motto: *Omne Solum Forti Patria Est* (To the Brave Man, Everything He Does Is for His Country).

Perhaps I am too young to do what Jefferson wants done, Meriwether Lewis thought. Yet his dream excites me. I wish I *could* be the man to carry out his grand plan.

2
Growing in Experience

TWO YEARS LATER Meriwether Lewis was one of the first to volunteer for service when President Washington called up the Virginia militia to quell the riots by men who objected to a new tax on whiskey. Lewis's brothers and sisters were growing up and able to help their mother during his absence. He was eager for change and adventure after years of family responsibility.

"I'll write to you often," he told his mother as he left Locust Hill on his favorite bay horse.

The Whiskey Rebellion lasted only a short time, but Lewis wrote his mother that he had decided to reenlist in a small army of occupation under General Daniel Morgan. He wrote that army life suited him. He enjoyed the companionship of fellow soldiers and had made many friends. He liked rambling through wilderness country. He was learning to live in camps and becoming a fine woodsman.

After another year he sent word that he had again refused discharge from the militia. He had been promoted to ensign. "I have a fine Philadelphia-made epaulet," he wrote. "Forgive me if I am causing you worry. I know the general idea is that the army is the school of debauchery, but, believe me, it has ever proven the school of experience and prudence to your affectionate son."

In August, 1795, Lewis's unit was sent to join the army of General "Mad Anthony" Wayne. He was stationed at headquarters when chiefs of many Indian tribes, recently defeated by Wayne's forces, paraded into camp to sign the peace treaty.

Ensign Lewis watched closely the chiefs of the Chippewas, Wyandots, Delawares, Shawnees, Ottawas, Kickapoos, Kaskaskias, and others. He had never before had a chance to observe the leaders of red men. He was impressed by the dignity and pride of the chiefs, even in defeat.

Dressed in their ceremonial robes, they came forward, one by one, to stand at the general's table and sign the paper "to put an end to a destructive war, to settle all controversies, and to restore harmony and friendly relations between the United States and the Indian tribes."

The chiefs looked to neither the left nor the right as they bent to make the sign of their tribe. Something in their faces made Lewis feel that they were still a people to be watched.

Men like these can be won only if we treat them honestly and fairly, he thought. Yet firmly, too, for they recognize and respect strength. Only a foolish man would underestimate these red men.

Sometime later he wrote his mother that he had been transferred to the Chosen Rifle Company of elite riflemen-sharpshooters. He knew his news would not surprise her, since he had always been a near-perfect shot. "But," he wrote happily, "the company is commanded by William Clark, younger brother to our neighbor, George Rogers Clark. William Clark is only four years older than I am, and we have become the best of friends."

A few months later Clark resigned from the service and went home to Kentucky. Lewis was transferred to the First U.S. Infantry Regiment. He wrote his mother that at last he was serving *with* Indians. He and a Wyandot, Captain Enos Coon, had gone on several lone missions into the wilderness together. He found the red soldier a first-rate woodsman and trusted companion.

While Lewis walked or rode in the wilderness, he had time to think and form his own beliefs. In the army, he felt he was responsible for the safety of his men and his country. In his personal life, he felt responsible for his own welfare and the welfare of his family.

After several years in the army, he asked for leave and went home to take care of business for his mother and his sisters and brothers. He visited and inspected his mother's property in Georgia. He rode horseback to Kentucky to lay claim to land inherited by the Marks children, Mary and John, from their father. Lewis had been named their guardian. He also bought 2,600 acres of land in Kentucky for himself before he returned to service.

From his new post, Fort Pickering on the Mississippi River, he wrote that he was learning more about Indian ways, since the fort bordered Cherokee country.

He was promoted to lieutenant and sent to the Indian frontier with Captain Claiborne's company. Three months later he became a captain and was appointed paymaster for his regiment.

This duty suited him exactly, he wrote his mother. He had always kept careful accounts, and he liked being constantly on the move. He traveled horseback or by dugout canoe to pay the scattered units of his regiment in many different forts and camps.

Captain Meriwether Lewis might have gone on enjoying the responsibility of his rambling army life indefinitely, but in February, 1801, he received an unexpected letter.

His former neighbor, Thomas Jefferson, had recently been elected President of the United States. He wanted Lewis to be his private secretary.

The astonished Lewis, who had not seen his older friend for several years, read President Jefferson's letter:

"The appointment to the Presidency has rendered it necessary for me to have a private secretary and in selecting one I have thought it important to respect not only his capacity to aid me in the private concerns of the household, but also to contribute to the mass of information which it is interesting to the Administration to acquire. Your knowledge of the Western Country, of the Army, and of all its interests and relations has rendered it desirable for public as well as private purposes that you should be engaged in that office. In point of profit it has little to offer; the salary being only 500 D. [per year], which would scarcely be more than an equivalent for your pay and rations, which you would be obliged to relinquish while withdrawn from active service, but retaining your rank and right to rise. But it would be an easier office, would make you known, and be known, to characters of influence in our Country, and give you the advantage of their wisdom. You would, of course, save also the expense of subsistence and lodgings, as you would be one of my family.

"If these or any other views which your own reflections may suggest should present the office of my private secretary as worthy of acceptance, you will make me happy in accepting it. It has been solicited by several, who will have no answer till I hear from you."

This was a request Lewis could not refuse. He wrote in answer, much more formally than he would have talked to his old neighbor:

"You have thought proper so far to honour me with your confidence as to express a wish that I should accept the place of your private secretary. I most cordially acquiesce, and with pleasure accept the office, nor were further motives necessary to induce my compliance than that you, Sir, should conceive that in the discharge of my duties of that office I could be serviceable to my country and useful to you."

April 1, 1801, Captain Lewis arrived in Washington after a long journey horseback over mud-bogged roads. President Jefferson had left the capital for a visit to Monticello to bring back some of his books and papers. Happily Lewis followed, and visited Locust Hill and his family again.

When President Jefferson and his young private secretary returned to Washington, they brought eleven efficient servants from Monticello to run the White House. Jefferson's wife was dead and his daughters were married. Yet he brought the Virginia way of life to the capital: hospitality, good food, and long conversations with the best of company.

Lewis arranged and helped plan the dinners and entertainment of the many guests at the White House. From Jefferson, Lewis had learned to be truly democratic. People of every kind were invited to the well-served, but informal, dinners. Every day Lewis learned from the talk of men who visited the President—scientists, doctors, foreign diplomats, and Congressmen from all parts of his own country.

Secretary Lewis wrote his mother that he enjoyed the company of the most accomplished men to be found anywhere. He also helped the President with affairs of state. He wrote letters. He carried personal messages that the President did not want entrusted to paper. He was making friends of his own in the capital too.

One afternoon when Lewis had been with the President for more than a year, Jefferson talked again about the grand plan he had first mentioned to his young neighbor nine years before.

Jefferson and Lewis walked in the White House garden after the last dinner guest had left. The President had something important on his mind, Lewis knew, for Jefferson ignored the pet mockingbird perched on his shoulder, even when the bird tweaked his ear to remind him that it was time for raisins.

"So little is known of the many tribes living up the Missouri River," the President began. "We do know these western Indians supply many fine furs to the British traders in the North. I see no reason why our own traders should not deal with the Indians along the Missouri."

Lewis waited. He knew Jefferson well. The President was interested in more than furs.

"I'm told the Missouri is a strong river," Jefferson went on, "possibly navigable north and west into the mountains. It leads into a very wide land which should be a part of the United States."

Lewis looked at the President quickly. He knew that Jefferson hoped to buy a part of the vast Louisiana Territory, which stretched west from the Mississippi River to the foot of the Rocky Mountains and north from the Gulf of Mexico to Canada. France was in the process of regaining, by treaty, the Territory of Louisiana from Spain.

The President knew how desperately France needed money, so he had sent agents to Napoleon to try to buy at least the city of New Orleans, which controlled the commerce up and down the Mississippi. Jefferson wanted to be sure that the United States retained the right to travel freely up and down the Mississippi, and that Western settlers would not be cut off from the Eastern states.

But now the President was speaking of something much more daring, navigation of the uncharted Missouri River whose western source no one knew.

"An intelligent officer," Jefferson continued, "with a few chosen men could explore the Missouri River country, even to the western Pacific Ocean. He could have talks with the Indian tribes along the way and get their permission for our traders to come into their territory and interchange articles the Indians need for the furs they trap. In short, he could make it plain to the Indians that we wish to live on neighborly terms with them. Even should we gain this territory, their lives would not be disturbed. Rather, we hope their lives might be better through the exchange of trade."

"Your grand plan!" Lewis said. "To be first to cross the continent and so lay claim to the Far West for the United States. After all this time, we may still do it ahead of the British."

"If we hurry," Jefferson said. "Britain has never given up hope of owning part of this continent. The British Government spends a great deal of money to back its fur traders throughout the Northwest, hoping to gain allies among the Indians. I hope our small Corps of Discovery can win the natives as our friends."

"When you first told me of your plan," Lewis said, "I wanted to go. You said I was too young. Sir, in the army I learned to deal with Indians. I am much more experienced—"

Jefferson smiled. "If you were not as nearly the ideal man as I could send," he said, "I would never have told you of my plan. You understand, Captain Lewis, that even now the expedition must be kept secret?"

Lewis nodded. He knew that Jefferson was meeting strong opposition from many congressmen, particularly Federalists, even to buying part of the Louisiana Territory. Some men, like Jefferson, saw the future value of the wild frontier. Others thought the territory would never be worth the battles with the Indians, the men, money, and trouble to protect it. One New Englander had written that Upper Louisiana Territory was a "tract of country which will not be inhabited by any other beings but bears and buffaloes for five hundred years."

How outraged these Federalists would be if they knew that Jefferson was sending an exploring party farther west of the territory into unmapped country! No one even knew how far it was to the Pacific Ocean.

"You would be gone possibly two years," President Jefferson said as he and Lewis returned to the White House.

They went to the map room. Jefferson pointed to the Missouri River, marked as far as it was known. Then he pointed to the western or Pacific shore. Only the mouth of the recently discovered Columbia River was indicated here.

"We know a little about the western coastline," he said, "from the observations of ships' captains and their crews. But no one has traveled inland to know how far the river goes. Perhaps there is a portage over the Rocky Mountains from the source of the Missouri River to the source of the Columbia. Such a portage could be only twenty miles. It could be a hundred miles or more. No man knows.

"Think what it would mean to America, if we could find a way to travel across the continent by water, with only a short portage between the great rivers?"

"If there is such a way," Lewis said, "I will do my best to find it."

"I'll ask Congress for a small appropriation of money," Jefferson said, "enough to continue supporting the Indian trading posts it has already established on the Mississippi. Thus we can keep the nature of your expedition confidential."

"Secretary of War Dearborn will have to be told," Lewis said.

Jefferson agreed. "And a few other men we trust. Your whole expense will be for arms, supplies, and gifts for the Indians to secure their cooperation," Jefferson planned. "Choose your own men, soldiers for the most part—men who are willing to undertake such an adventure for regular army pay. Members of the expedition will be rewarded, upon their return, by grants of land equal to those given to the Revolutionary soldiers for their service."

"How shall I recruit men secretly?" Lewis wondered aloud.

"Say as little as possible of the adventure," Jefferson advised him. "If questions are asked, indicate that you are planning a trip up the Mississippi River. Thus you can buy supplies without suspicion."

"Yes," Lewis agreed, "but the men must be told their destination before we start, so they can refuse to go if they choose. This adventure can be accomplished only with men of stout heart."

"I leave it in your hands," Jefferson said. "Choose whom you will to accompany you. I need not tell you how carefully you must prepare for such a journey."

"I'll begin at once," Lewis promised.

3
Secret Preparations

MERIWETHER LEWIS believed that it was wrong for a man to anticipate evil or expect an adverse outcome to an undertaking. But, he reasoned, a man is expected to use foresight and do everything he can to prevent troubles.

For months Lewis thought of little except the requirements for his journey. He planned and worked constantly on solving the problems he might meet in carrying out the purposes of the expedition.

He knew how to survive in the wilderness. His army experience proved that he could lead men. All his life he had been observant and interested in the trees, flowers, and geography of the country around him. But President Jefferson wanted scientific accounts of the wildlife of the unexplored West. "Botany I rank with the most valuable sciences," Jefferson had said.

Lewis knew that he needed advice and tutoring from the most learned men in the United States. He had met some of these men. Most of them were friends of Jefferson. The President wrote to trusted men telling them of the expedition and asking them to assist Lewis and keep his secret.

As a result Lewis went to Philadelphia to study with professors there, among them a naturalist, a scientist who taught Lewis how to set a course by the stars, how to figure longitude and latitude, and helped him choose the instruments to take with him. Dr. Benjamin Rush made up a list of herbs and medicines for Lewis to use in treating himself and his men in sickness. An ornithologist, Wilson, asked Lewis to make up a list of birds that he saw in the West. Every man with whom Lewis studied asked Lewis to learn, on the journey, about the professor's particular interest and to report to him later.

Henry Dearborn, Jefferson's Secretary of War, asked Lewis to list the Indian tribes of the West, to estimate their strength, discover whether or not they were friendly to the United States, and to make a list of the trade goods that the Indians needed most. Sometimes it seemed to Lewis that he should be several men to do all that people wanted him to do.

He collected maps from many sources, both American and French maps, showing as much of the continent as was known then. He also had a cartographer draw a blank map so he could put in any new geographical information that he discovered on the trip.

Lewis wrote innumerable letters in order to secure men and supplies, being careful not to describe his actual destination.

He went to Harper's Ferry to look over the Government's military supplies and choose the rifles, tomahawks, and knives he needed. He also got lead, powder, and other necessities here. He drew supplies from the Schuylkill Arsenal in Philadelphia—warm durable clothing, blankets, and camp equipment.

Whatever he could not get from army supplies, he bought or ordered from merchants. For months he gathered foods that would keep, medicines, spyglasses, surveyor's compass, poles and chains, microscope, slates, pencils, pens, ink, writing paper, and journals. He selected books to take: one each of botany, mineral-

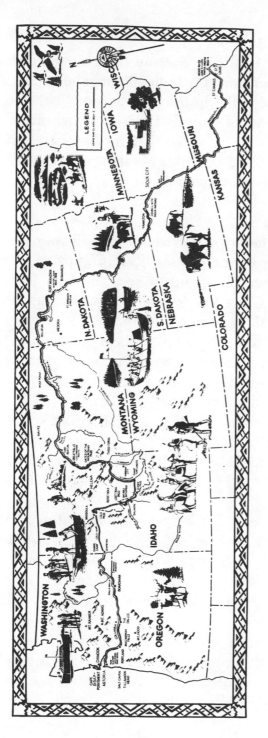

Meriwether Lewis and his partner, William Clark, with their band of "stout, healthy, unmarried young men, accustomed to the woods," mapped the Louisiana Purchase and the Western Territories for claim by the United States. They struggled up the Missouri, through uncharted and hostile Indian land, over the Great Falls and the frozen Rockies, to the Snake River and down the Columbia to the Pacific Coast.

ogy, astronomy, and Dr. Rush's *Rules of Health.* And he bought a large supply of presents for the Indians whom he hoped to win as friends.

So much depended upon Captain Lewis as leader of the expedition that Jefferson and he decided that another man should be chosen to assist him—a man capable of taking over the responsibility of the Corps of Discovery if anything happened to Lewis on the way.

Jefferson left the choice of partner to Lewis, who knew exactly the man he wanted. He wrote to red-haired William Clark with whom he had served in the Chosen Rifle Company of sharpshooters. Lewis warned his friend to keep the plan secret and offered to share with Clark any rewards and honors as freely as they would share the dangers of the journey.

In one letter to Clark he wrote, "If there is anything which would induce you to participate with me in its fatigues, its dangers, and its honors, there is no man on earth with whom I should feel equal pleasure in sharing them as yourself."

William Clark answered, "My friend, I can assure you that no man lives with whom I would prefer to undertake and share the difficulties of such a trip than yourself." Clark ended a later letter with the promise to go: "My friend, I join you with hand and heart."

Lewis then wrote asking Clark if he could recruit in Kentucky "several stout, healthy, unmarried, young men, accustomed to the woods and capable of bearing bodily fatigue to a pretty considerable degree." He added that they must be more than woodsmen and hunters. They must be willing to work at any task that came to the adventurers.

After more than half a year of preparation, Captain Meriwether Lewis was ready to leave Washington for Pittsburgh, on the Ohio, where he had ordered a keelboat built. The keelboat would carry his supplies down the Ohio River to the Mississippi, from which he could reach the Missouri River.

Before he left on July 4, 1803, he wrote his mother that he had hoped to get home to see her, but delays by some of his suppliers had already put him behind schedule. He must get down the Ohio River before the low water of summer made it impossible. He planned to spend the winter in St. Louis, so he would be ready to begin the expedition as soon as the ice broke on the Missouri River in the spring of 1804.

"The charge of this expedition is as honorable to myself as it is to my country," he wrote his mother. "For its fatigues I find myself perfectly prepared, nor do I doubt my health and strength of constitution to bear me through it. I go with the most perfect preconviction in my mind of returning safe, and hope, therefore, that you will not suffer yourself to indulge in anxiety for my safety."

Captain Lewis borrowed horses and a wagon from the army to transport his supplies over the long rough road to Pittsburgh, which he reached on July 15. As soon as he had sent Jefferson a note of his safe arrival, he went to the Ohio River dock to see the keelboat he had ordered to be made. It was evening. The boatwright might have gone home, but Lewis would recognize his boat from any others.

It was his own special design, a large bargelike boat with ten-foot decks at stern and bow and a large square sail. There was to be a forecastle with a cabin on top for shelter, and lockers in the center that could be raised to protect the men from Indian arrows in case of an attack. He had even ordered a tarpaulin to fit over the entire storage area to keep the supplies dry.

Lewis walked along the river front searching among the boats at the docks. It was growing dark, but he could see that there was no such boat tied there. He was alarmed, then reasoned that the boatwright might have taken his keelboat on the river for a test run. Or it might be on winches inside the warehouse. The keelboat had been promised for the twentieth of July. The boatwright still had four days to complete it. He must be patient.

The next morning Lewis returned. There was still no activity at the warehouse. He entered and found a man asleep on a cot in the back room. When awakened, the man sounded sick or drunk, as he offered excuses. Lewis could scarcely believe what the boatwright was saying. His promised keelboat was scarcely begun.

For six weeks Lewis spent most of his time overseeing the building of the keelboat. He threatened, persuaded, and urged the workmen to hurry.

Old-time rivermen at the docks told Lewis that he had better buy a secondhand boat and be on his way. His boat would be hung up, high and dry, if he did not get out of Pittsburgh at once. A boat that size would never get through the low water of August.

Lewis knew he must have a good boat to carry the large store of supplies for his expedition. Daily he came and stood over the workmen until the keelboat was finished at seven in the morning on the last day of August. He had the boat loaded in three hours.

He told the rivermen, who had assembled to see him off, that the river would not stop him. The water was very low, but he was determined to go on, even if he made no more than a mile a day.

"Even should I not be able to make a greater speed than a boat's length per day," he said as he cast off.

On the trip to Louisville, Kentucky, Lewis and his eleven men spent much of their travel in the water. They pushed their keelboat over sandbars and driftwood barriers. Often they had to unload the boat and lift it over, then reload again. A few times they were able to set sail and move along briskly. More often Lewis was forced to walk to some farm or village in search of horses or oxen to pull the boat off ground.

At Louisville he was delighted to find William Clark and several recruits waiting to join him. Lewis told his friend that he and his men had walked as much of the Ohio River as they had sailed it.

When the boat reached the deeper waters of the Mississippi and started upriver toward St. Louis, the two young leaders spent much of their time discussing plans for the adventure ahead. Lewis asked Clark to take charge of the small fleet of boats they would assemble. "You are the better sailor, I think," he said.

And he told Clark that Jefferson had been overjoyed by France's recent response to the offer of the United States to buy New Orleans. Napoleon had needed money so much that he had sold the *entire* Louisiana Territory for fifteen million dollars.

"That's good news," Clark said. "I wasn't looking forward to crossing Spanish territory, knowing how suspicious Spain is of any move west by the United States. And I understand that the Spanish have not yet turned over St. Louis and upper Lousiana to France."

"Unfortunately," Lewis said, "communication is unbelievably slow in the wilderness country. Colonel Delassus, the Commandant at St. Louis, claims that he has never received official notice from Spain that the Lousiana Territory was traded back to France."

Clark whistled. "I hope he knows it by now," he said. "And that he also knows that America, in turn, bought Louisiana from France, or we won't be staying this winter in St. Louis."

"We'll stop at Fort Kaskaskia on the American side of the river," Lewis told him. "I'll go alone to St. Louis with a letter of introduction from Jefferson. You and the men can follow later if the Commandant grants us permission. I plan to ask Postmaster

John Hay at Cahokia to come with me and interpret. He speaks French well, as does the Spanish Commandant."

Clark smiled. "I might have known you would think of everything," he said.

Thorough as Lewis was, he met disappointment when he crossed the river to St. Louis on December 8, 1803. Through interpreters, Commandant Don Carlos Delassus listened to Captain Lewis with deep courtesy.

At last he answered, "I believe you are an honest young man, Captain Lewis. You are certainly pleasing and likable. You will be a welcome guest in the homes of St. Louis this winter. You alone. Not your troops."

"My force is small," Lewis said. "Surely so few men could be no threat."

Commandant Delassus was said to be a stern official, respected but dreaded by the people of St. Louis. Yet Lewis liked him at once and Delassus liked the captain.

"You are a courageous young man," Delassus said. "The letter from your President Jefferson assures me that you are harmless to Spain. That you are leading a peaceful exploration to discover a water passage to the western sea.

"Personally I wish you well on your expedition. But my orders from the Spanish Government are clear. I am never, under any circumstances, to admit foreigners into the interior of the provinces. I cannot grant you permission to ascend the Missouri River."

Lewis saw more clearly than before how important his expedition was. Jefferson had been right. Americans could never move west freely unless the United States gained the land from sea to sea.

Immediately Lewis sent a letter to William Clark waiting across the river on the American side. He asked Clark to choose a campsite to winter nearby. Clark picked a spot on Wood River about eighteen miles from St. Louis.

Except for short visits to the camp, Captain Lewis spent the winter in St. Louis to learn from the people living in the stone houses and log cabins of the town. He was well liked and invited everywhere. The Spanish and French citizens called him, "Captain Merry" or sometimes, "Merry Weather."

The women smiled and danced with him. The men answered his many questions about the west and the Indians, or about agriculture and trade.

Since it was difficult to speak with citizens without an interpreter, Lewis had printed a questionnaire in their languages. He asked for a list of animals, birds, and fishes found in the streams they knew. He asked if they had lead, iron, or other minerals. He asked to borrow maps or journals kept by private traders and trappers. Carefully he copied any information he thought helpful to send on to Jefferson.

And at last, on March 9, 1804, Captain Meriwether Lewis acted as President Jefferson's personal envoy in accepting the Territory of Louisiana for America. Lewis, dressed in his best army uniform trimmed with lace, accompanied Captain Amos Stoddard of the United States Army. Stoddard had been authorized to accept the territory *for* France, then immediately receive it *from* France for his own country.

Captain Lewis, standing at attention with the officers and soldiers of three nations, listened to Commandant Delassus' last brief speech to the assembled people of St. Louis. "I am about to deliver up this post and its dependencies. The flag under which you have been protected for almost thirty-six years is to be withdrawn."

Delassus and Stoddard signed the formal document of transfer. Lewis witnessed it with two others.

At the end of the ceremony, the Spanish soldiers filed out, the Spanish flag came down. In a courteous answer to the wishes of the old French settlers of St. Louis, the United States had agreed that the flag of France would fly over the city for one day. Now French soldiers came forward and raised their tricolor.

The next day Lewis returned to take part in the ceremony of raising the Stars and Stripes. He was deeply moved and wished that President Jefferson could be there to see the troops of the United States take possession of the rich territory Jefferson had worked with such vision to secure.

"I must do my part now," Lewis said to himself. "Then America will be as wide and free as Jefferson dreamed."

4
On Their Way

CAPTAINS LEWIS AND CLARK decided to meet and begin their expedition from St. Charles, a town of about one hundred houses settled by the French, a short distance up the Missouri River from St. Louis. Clark brought the men and supplies from Wood River camp. They arrived on the "fleet"—the keelboat and two pirogues, long French canoes hollowed from tree trunks, one painted red, one white.

Captain Lewis rode horseback with many of his friends from St. Louis. These friends gave a farewell party for the leaders of the expedition. Long before the party was over, the people of the town, every man, woman, and child, lined the bank of the river. They brought picnic food, which they shared with the soldiers and rivermen before the men boarded the boats.

In midafternoon of May 21, 1804, Captain Lewis shook hands with Captain Stoddard and his other friends at the landing. He boarded the keelboat with Scammon, the Newfoundland dog he had bought for a hunting companion. The expedition was ready to go.

"Sail!" Lewis called. Clark motioned for the boats to move off, while the people cheered and waved good-by.

Lewis stood at the bow with his hand on Scammon's black head. He had spent almost every waking moment for more than a year in preparing for this journey. The men were carefully chosen for their courage and the kind of work they could do, the best men Clark and he could find.

With Clark was his black servant, York, the largest, strongest man among them. York was cheerful and a good hunter too.

Rowing the two pirogues were Baptiste Deschamps and nine French rivermen from St. Louis and Kaskaskia, who had agreed to go as far upriver as the first winter camp, probably the Mandan Indian villages.

Corporal Richard Warfington and six privates from the U.S. Army accompanied the party. They were to stay with the explorers until they passed the dangerous Sioux country, then these soldiers planned to turn back.

Captain Lewis was particularly pleased with a number of the permanent members of his corps, men who had agreed to go all the way to the Pacific. First was George Drouillard, his scout, interpreter, and chief hunter. Tall, straight, with black hair and eyes, Drouillard was half Shawnee and half French. He knew Indian woodcraft and the Indian sign language that most tribes understood.

There was John Colter, a fellow Virginian the same age as Lewis, who had been a ranger on the frontier.

William Werner from Kentucky was a good cook.

John Shields was a boatwright as well as a blacksmith and the best gunsmith among them. Alexander Willard from New Hampshire and William Bratton were gunsmiths too.

Joseph and Reuben Fields, two brothers from Kentucky, were the best of woodsmen and soldiers.

Three sergeants, Charles Floyd and his cousin, Nathaniel Pryor, and John Ordway, were intelligent young officers.

Bearded Patrick Gass was the carpenter-soldier, Silas Goodrich an expert fisherman. George Shannon from Pennsylvania, only eighteen, was the youngest among them and as eager to go as Lewis had been at his age.

Private George Gibson played the violin. Lewis knew that Gibson and another fiddler, one-eyed riverman Peter Cruzatte, would help lift the spirits of the men of the expedition with their music. He counted on them, too, to entertain and please the Indians whom they would meet.

Captain Clark had agreed to make surveys and draw maps, as well as take charge of the boats.

Lewis had set for himself the responsibility of commander, the tasks of doctor, explorer, scientist, and journalist. He intended to walk along the banks of the river much of the way, and to explore inland on foot whenever possible. Each night he would write an account of the country through which they passed to send, later, to Jefferson. He had asked all the men who could write to keep diaries, too, so that nothing important would be overlooked. Lewis, Clark, and four of the soldiers had agreed to keep records of any new plant, animal, or unusual happening along the way.

Day by day the boats moved up the Missouri River, contending with fog, floating islands, swift currents, and twisted channels among hidden sandbars. They managed to clear such traps by poling, or by what the French rivermen called cordelling, men walking the riverbanks pulling the boat with a cordelle, or rope.

Sometimes the boats were damaged and they had to stop for repairs.

Once Lewis wrote that they camped in a beautiful nature-garden. Wild plums and apples grew along the riverbanks. He picked wild raspberries. Herds of deer fed among the young willows, and the men had plenty of deer meat to eat.

His journal listed less happy events too. Joseph Fields was bitten by a rattlesnake. Lewis tied a poultice of bark and gunpowder on the wound and Fields lived. One man lost his gun when a pirogue caught on a snag and spilled him into the river. Another cut his leg on jagged rock. York almost lost his sight when sand was accidentally thrown into his eyes while the men fought quicksand. Lewis treated York's inflamed eyes with Dr. Rush's medicine, and they healed.

The heat of summer grew so unbearable that the men had to rest in the afternoons to keep from collapsing. The river water that they had to drink was warm and muddy. They developed boils and dysentery. Lewis treated them with Dr. Rush's pills and bled them for sunstroke. When the scorching sun went down, on the prairies, the nights were often cool, but the men were kept awake by hordes of mosquitoes.

In June the expedition camped to wait out a storm and to repair the keelboat that had been snagged by old hidden trees under the chocolate-colored water. Lewis saw a raft coming downstream and hailed the man aboard it.

The raft was piled high with furs and with bladders of buffalo grease and tallow. The trader, Pierre Dorion, was on his way to sell his furs at a trading post near St. Louis, he said.

Lewis invited Dorion to supper and asked him about the Indians ahead.

Dorion said that he had traded with the southern Sioux for twenty years. The Sioux Nation was made up of many bands, or tribes, of Indians. Among those Lewis would meet were the Da-kotas, Yanktons, Ogalalas, and Tetons. Right now they were at peace, spending the summer on buffalo hunts, but the tribes often made war on each other over trivial offenses.

"The southern Sioux may allow you to pass without trouble," Dorion said, "but the northern Teton Sioux are proud, warlike, and jealous of their territory. They have stopped every trader's boat going upriver and stolen the cargo."

"I'll pay you," Lewis said, "to go back with us to meet the Sioux. They know you, and you speak their language. You can help me persuade some of their chiefs to go to Washington and visit President Jefferson."

Dorion looked at Lewis in surprise. "Why would your President want Indian chiefs as guests?"

"Jefferson knows that the Sioux are the most powerful nation on the Missouri," Lewis explained. "The President asked me to send chiefs from any tribe. He wants the chiefs to come and see for themselves that America is a great but peaceful nation, that we are well able to keep the promises we make to them."

Dorion agreed to go with the expedition, but only until they met the southern Sioux.

After supper, Clark told Lewis that the trapper seemed as wild as the Indians and added, "I doubt that he will be much help."

"You may be right," Lewis said, "but we must make friends of the Indians in any way possible."

When the boats reached the valley where the Platte River joined the Missouri, Lewis again called a halt to rest his ex-hausted men. They found plums to eat and gooseberries and chokecherries. Lewis wrote that chokecherries puckered his mouth but tasted good to the fruit-hungry men. They stored the cherries in a barrel of whiskey for winter use.

After more than two months of travel they had not come upon

a tribe or village of Indians. Lewis wondered if the natives could be avoiding the expedition. Dorion said the Indians were on the move, hunting buffalo, this time of year.

Lewis sent Drouillard and Cruzatte to scout for Indians. Finally Drouillard returned with an Oto Indian hunter he had found on the plains. Lewis sent the Indian to his tribe to invite the Oto chiefs to meet at a council on the high bluffs above the river.

On August 2, six minor chiefs of the Oto and Missouri tribes came to the council bluff with some of their warriors. Lewis saluted them with the bow gun and cannon on the keelboat. He shook hands with them and invited them to return the next day for talks.

He prepared a reception for the Indians on the open bank of the river, where his men could keep a careful guard. The Indians returned with watermelons, which everyone ate with roast meat and cornmeal cakes provided by the expedition. After the feast, the Indians sat on the grass under an awning the men had made by stretching the mainsail of the keelboat over four high cornerposts.

Lewis stood, ready to speak to them through Dorion and Drouillard. On a blanket beside him were gifts—medals for the chiefs, a canister of gunpowder, carrots, or ropes, of twisted tobacco. In his hand Lewis held the American flag, representing the seventeen states of the Union.

"Children," Lewis said, "I have been sent by the Great Chief of America."

The Indians listened intently, for they could see that this man had honored them with careful preparation of the place and the words he was about to say.

"I was sent to inform all the nations of red men who inhabit the Missouri that a great council was lately held between the

Great Chief of America and your fathers, the French and the Spaniards. It was agreed that all white men inhabiting the waters of the Missouri and Mississippi should now obey the commands of this Great American Chief."

Lewis told the Indians that they had nothing to fear from their change of protectors. The Great Chief of America gladly adopted them.

Then Lewis added, "He has commanded us, his war chiefs, to undertake this long journey with great labor and much expense, in order to council with you and his other red children on the Troubled Waters. He has sent us to make the road of peace between himself and his red people residing here, to enquire into the nature of their wants and, on our return, to inform him of them, that he may make the necessary arrangements for their relief.

"He has further commanded us to tell you that when you accept this flag and medals, you accept herewith his hand of friendship, which will never be withdrawn from your nation as long as you continue to follow the councils which he may command his chiefs to give you.

"You are to live in peace with all white men, neither wage war against the red men, your neighbors, for they are equally his children and he is bound to protect them."

Lewis warned the Indians not to obstruct the passage of any boat coming or going on the Missouri and to do no harm to the traders who would come to them under the protection of this, their Great Chief's flag. He set the Stars and Stripes on a staff in the ground so the Indians could see it flutter in the breeze.

"I am not a trader," Lewis told them. "My journey is too long for me to carry many presents. But American traders will come later. They will bring blankets, guns, powder, and all other goods you want in exchange for the furs you trap and hunt.

"The Great Chief wishes your chiefs to visit him in Washington," he added. "He will furnish you with guides and horses for the journey. And he promises to return you safely to your tribe when your visit is over."

Lewis was pleased when the chiefs, in turn, rose and spoke eloquently. They promised to follow the advice of their new Great American Chief. They would consider a visit to him. It was a long way. They must think about it. Later the Oto and Missouri visitors left the camp with smiling farewells.

That evening Lewis told Clark, as they sat beside the campfire recording events of the day in their journals, "I hope all my speeches will be as well received as this one."

Clark grinned. "You were persuasive. No one would know this was your first council speech."

Sergeant Ordway looked up from his writing. "Yes," he said, "they appeared to be glad that they got freed from all other powers."

In mid-August, Lewis called another halt so his men could rest and fish. With willow drags, they brought in more than a thousand fish of many kinds, which Lewis described in his journals. The men were more interested in eating the fresh fish, baked and fried, a welcome relief from their regular diet of cornmeal and grease, with occasional roast meat from game shot on the prairies by their hunters.

Lewis, eager to meet tribes of the Sioux nation, set fire to grass along the river's bank, a sign that Indians used to bring in other tribes to council. No Sioux answered, but the head Chief of the Otos came. He brought with him lesser chiefs who had not attended the meeting at Council Bluffs.

On the eighteenth of August, Lewis celebrated his thirtieth birthday with another ceremony. He repeated his speech. The Indians stayed two nights and danced for their hosts.

Lewis was watching their leaps and cries around the campfire, to the sound of drumbeats and Cruzatte's fiddle, when one of his men came and told him that Sergeant Floyd was very ill. Quickly he went to the tent shelter Floyd's friends had made for him.

He examined the young man. Floyd's stomach was rigid with colic, and Lewis could feel no pulse in his wrist. He called Clark. Together they treated Floyd with stomach pills and stayed by him all night to comfort him.

Sergeant Floyd's death saddened the whole camp. Lewis tried to think what else he might have done, but the sickness had been too sudden and violent for medicine to help.

Lewis read a burial service while the men stood at attention. Later they cut and trimmed a new cedar post to mark Floyd's grave on the bluff.

That evening Lewis wrote a letter to the young man's family. He would send it back with Corporal Warfington, who would return to St. Louis with the keelboat when the expedition made its winter camp at the Mandan villages. Lewis had learned from trader Dorion that the river above the Mandans was not deep enough to float the keelboat.

We have perhaps seven or eight weeks, Lewis thought, through Sioux Territory, before we reach the Mandan Indians.

He was determined to make the most of every day before he had to stop and build a winter fort. But the next few days Lewis was ill. Many of his men were sick with boils and stomach cramps.

Lewis gave orders from his bed of blankets on the ground. He sent Dorion and Pryor out with three Omaha Indians whom Drouillard had brought into camp after a hunting trip. He asked them to find the Yankton Sioux and invite the Sioux to a council.

By the time Dorion and Pryor returned with about seventy-five Yankton Sioux warriors, Lewis had regained most of his strength.

Lewis pleased the Indians by inviting them to perform one of their dances. They stretched a deerskin over a keg to make a drum. Indians beat upon it while other warriors leaped around the campfire and shook rattles made of dried rawhide filled with pebbles.

Lewis gave his men gifts to toss into the ring of dancers as a show of applause. The Indians danced faster and more joyfully as they snatched up the presents—carrots of tobacco, small tinkling bells, knives, and beads.

For his part Lewis gave his speech from the Great Chief of America. He shot his rifle into a tree and astonished the Indians with the precise holes he put in the tree trunk at a great distance. He gave the lesser chiefs tobacco and medals. To the Grand Chief of the Yankton Sioux, he presented a U.S. officer's lace-trimmed coat and a cocked hat with a red feather in it.

Then he smoked a pipe of peace with the chiefs. Before they left, they warned him of the northern Sioux by making a sign of cutting the throat.

"They are not as we," the Grand Chief said. "The Teton Sioux have turned back all French and Spanish traders who would go up the Missouri. They will stop you."

Having met and won the Yankton Sioux through whose country he was passing, Lewis said good-by to Dorion, who turned back to sell his furs. Now Lewis left the boats often to go on scientific walking explorations alone. On his back he carried a pack with blanket, rifle, and spyglass. He wore a dirk in his belt and carried an espontoon, a short staff tipped with a steel lance point. Sometimes he returned to the river at night and met the boats. Other times he went so far inland that he slept overnight on the prairie.

Often he took his dog, Scammon, with him. The big dog obeyed his master's orders not to bark when they saw herds of antelope, deer, and buffalo. Scammon only whined impatiently when Lewis watched the strange animals through his spyglass, observing details to describe in his journal.

Late in September, Lewis was on the keelboat when three curious Indian boys swam alongside it. Clark invited them aboard. Through Drouillard, Lewis questioned them. The boys said that they came from a large Teton Sioux village not far ahead. Lewis sent his scout to invite the Teton chiefs to a council.

Lewis located the council site on the riverbank in the open and placed guards. He set up the American flag. When the chiefs arrived, he greeted them with handshakes.

The Teton Sioux remained silent and hostile. They listened to Lewis's speech and said nothing. He offered the pipe of peace. The Indians passed the pipe from man to man. Each warrior blew only one quick insolent puff of smoke into the circle.

Hiding his uneasiness, Lewis presented medals and an American flag to the Grand Chief and four lesser chiefs. They scarcely looked at the gifts, but demanded to go aboard the keelboat.

Lewis agreed and took them out in a pirogue. He hoped this hospitality would please them. On board the keelboat, they asked for whiskey. Lewis gave each chief a fourth of a glass. They seemed no more friendly than before.

Clark told Lewis quietly that Teton braves had just stolen a
horse from John Colter, a horse Colter had bought from the
Yankton Sioux. Lewis asked the chiefs to have the horse returned. They frowned and seemed not to understand.

Lewis realized that Drouillard's sign language was limited
when the scout tried to interpret the conversations exactly. He
wished that Dorion was here.

Looking at the scowling Indians, Lewis said that it was time for
them to go ashore. They were openly staring at everything on the
keelboat. Covetously they peered into the forecastle.

Finally the chiefs stepped into the pirogue. Clark and several
men rowed them ashore. As the pirogue touched the riverbank,
Teton warriors caught its mast. One of the chiefs grabbed Clark's
arm. Indians surrounded the pirogue and took arrows from their
quivers.

Clark and his men showed no fear. They lifted their guns, but
held their fire. Lewis ordered the men on the keelboat to turn
their guns on the Indians too.

He hoped he would not have to order "fire" to save his men
ashore. He was here to make friends. After a difficult moment,
the Grand Chief turned from looking down the gunbarrels. He
pushed between his warriors and the pirogue. Clark and his men
rowed back to the keelboat.

Lewis ordered the expedition boats upriver a mile and
mounted double guards for the night. Hundreds of Teton warriors followed along the banks of the river. They beckoned to
Lewis and Clark, waving a buffalo robe in sign language.

Drouillard said, "They say they want to be friends. To honor
such brave men. Come to their council house."

Lewis and Clark talked together. They doubted the Indians'
offer of friendship. But they must still pass the Teton village
ahead. The warriors were testing them. If the expedition did not

show determination and fearlessness now, the Indians would believe these white men were like all the others they had robbed
and turned back or killed.

"We have no choice but to go ashore as their guests," Lewis
said.

Clark agreed, although two men against a whole village was
pretty long odds, he said.

That night the two officers sat in the Teton village, smoked the
pipe of peace and listened to long speeches by the chiefs. Nearby
Teton squaws danced late to music from Indian drums.

A strange way of showing friendship, Lewis thought, as he
glanced at the scalp locks hanging in the council lodge and
around the waists of his Indian hosts. Most of the scalp locks
were long, coarse black hair, but there was light-brown hair, too,
like no Indian hair Lewis had seen.

It was very late when Lewis and Clark stood up to return to
camp. The Tetons must have admired such cool confidence and
courage, for they let them go.

Yet when Lewis gave orders the next morning to move on up
the river, the Indians again gathered on the riverbank. They had
stolen the keelboat's anchor, by swimming the river in the darkness. Now they waded into the water to catch the towrope. They
made threatening motions for the boat to go back. "Not pass,"
they shouted. "More presents."

Lewis pulled on board one of the young Indians who swam
along side of the keelboat. He sent back a message, short and
clear, so the Tetons could not misunderstand it.

"If you wish peace, stay where you are. If you try to stop us,
my men and I are able to defend ourselves, and we will."

With these words Lewis left the Sioux nation behind.

October was a third gone when the boats came to a village of
Arikaras living on a three-mile-long island in the river. These In-

dians welcomed the expedition and gave them bread made from corn and beans, which they grew. Lewis was particularly interested in some wild beans that the Arikaras took from the burrows of the white-footed mice who gathered them on the prairie. The wild beans tasted like peanuts, he thought.

After eating with the chiefs, Lewis gave his speech.

The Arikaras answered him. "We will consider your invitation to visit the Great Chief of America. Such a long journey is dangerous and not to be undertaken lightly."

Lewis noticed that the nights were cold now. The trees and grass were often white with frost in the mornings. Ice would soon freeze on the river. The Arikaras told him that the next Indian villages would be those of the Mandans, where he planned to build a winter fort.

5
Fort Mandan

ON CHRISTMAS EVE, 1804, Captain Lewis watched men drive the last picket into the stockade that enclosed the expedition's winter fort. His men had begun to cut down trees with axes on the second of November, as soon as Captain Clark had found the site on the bank of the Missouri a few miles from the two Mandan villages. Here were tall cottonwoods for logs. Up and down the riverbanks were stones to build chimneys. A high bluff, or rimrock, protected them from bitter winter winds.

In the shape of a U, the men had built eight log barrack rooms, two storehouses, and a smokehouse to cure meat. Captain Lewis ordered guards on duty at the fort day and night, although the Mandan Indians had become friendly after a less than enthusiastic welcome when the expedition arrived.

As Lewis walked back to the room he shared with Clark, he smiled, remembering the Indians' change of attitude from suspicion to deep interest. The Mandans had been cool toward the strangers, but their curiosity overcame them, and they gathered to watch the men work. They were greatly impressed to see the powerful York lift tree trunks which any two men might have found too heavy.

The tall, handsome Mandans, with light-brown skin, had crowded around the first black man they had ever seen. One chief grew bold enough to rub York's arm to see if the color would come off, as if the blackness itself held the secret of York's strength.

York delighted in their half-fearful curiosity. He had made faces and grunted like a wild animal. The Indians had drawn back until York laughed. After some hesitation the Indians saw the joke and laughed too. They surged around him in admiration. The black man outdid himself in lifting logs for their applause. Several Mandan chiefs had urged York to remain with their tribe as a son-in-law, but York was too proud of his part in the expedition. He laughed and said that Captain Clark could not get along without him.

The Indians' greatest admiration was for the blacksmith, Shields. Daily, men, women, and children stood near the forge in the fort's compound and watched the bellows in astonishment. The Mandans brought baskets of corn, squash, and other foods to trade for the blacksmith's skill in fashioning arrow tips, war axes, and iron tools for them. Lewis had given a rusty iron stove from the keelboat for Shields to make the articles the Indians wanted.

The Indians loved Cruzatte's and Gibson's fiddles too. They often danced along with the men of the expedition. For no matter how hard the men worked, they were ready in the evening to sing and dance to the fiddles. The Indians laughed and whooped when they watched the white men's strange jigging, or swinging of partners in square dances.

Now Captain Lewis reached the barracks and entered. He spoke to Clark, who sat before the fireplace, "How is your neck?"

Clark rubbed the back of his neck, which had been so stiff and sore after a severe cold that he could scarcely move his head. "Could be better," he admitted.

Lewis took two stones, heated in the coals in the fire, and wrapped them in a piece of flannel. "Better warm your neck again with these," he said. "At least tomorrow is a day of rest."

He had given the men Christmas Day off and told the cook to use an extra ration of dried apples and flour to add variety to their usual dinner of buffalo meat. Captain Clark had given the men a present of brandy.

Lewis wanted the men to enjoy their merrymaking without any incidents between them and the Indians. He had asked the chiefs to keep their people away from the fort on Christmas Day.

Although the Mandans had grown used to crowding into the compound every day, they respected the white man's "Big Medicine Day" and only watched from afar.

Lewis knew that the Indians must have been filled with curiosity when they heard the cannon and guns fire on Christmas morning and saw the flag of the United States raised over the fort for the first time. They must have been even more tempted to come to the gate when they heard Cruzzate's fiddle, the tambourine, and the horn, mixed with clapping and singing and the clomping of feet as the men danced all day.

With the fort completed, Lewis turned to many other tasks that had to be done. He was forever on the move, watching the health of his men, seeing to the equipment. He was particularly concerned with the condition of the boats, frozen solid in the river with ice piling higher about them in every storm. He spent many days hunting so the men could have meat to eat.

Often Lewis went alone, sometimes with Drouillard or other hunters. The snow was so deep they walked on snowshoes as much as twenty miles a day. In below-zero temperatures, they slept rolled in buffalo robes on the ground. They hunted for days at a time and cached their buffalo and deer meat in trees to keep the wolves from eating it. Later they returned with men and horses from the fort and with Indian dogsleds, to pack the frozen meat home.

Lewis spent many days visiting the Mandan villages. He was always interested in learning anything new. Black Cat, head chief of the Upper Mandan Village, invited Lewis to supper in his large earthen lodge. The captain accepted, since he had found Black Cat to be as honest, intelligent, and trustworthy as any man he had ever met. Lewis took a new interpreter with him, a man named Charbonneau, who had been living with the Indians but had moved to the fort with his Indian wife after the expedition hired him.

Sitting on a buffalo robe on the dirt floor of the lodge, Lewis and Black Cat smoked an Indian pipe, passing it back and forth in silence. Lewis took stock of the furnishings of the lodge so that he could describe them in his journal for Jefferson: a fire pit in the center, cache pits in the floor to store foodstuffs and weapons, a stone grinding basin for corn. The circular earth walls were shored up by timbers. Against the walls were low bunks covered with buffalo robes. The horns of a bull buffalo had been placed on a tall stick to make a family altar.

Black Cat saw Lewis looking at the bowl of food placed at the foot of the altar stick. He said, "We, too, have our Big Medicine Days. We honor the buffalo that he will never leave us hungry."

Then Black Cat warned the captain that English and French traders, who had recently come to visit the camp and the fort, had really come to see how strong the American expedition was.

"The English traders said they will buy all our furs," Black Cat told him. "They do not want us to let the American traders come. They give many presents to the Sioux and the Cree to attack you. Better you should not go on west in the spring."

"Thank you," Lewis answered, "but we have not come sixteen hundred miles to turn back now."

Their conversation was interrupted when Indian women brought four horses into the lodge, so nearly filling it that Lewis wondered how anyone would be able to sleep without being switched by a horse's tail or kept awake by the horse's snorting. The women dumped bundles of bare cottonwood twigs on the floor for the horses to eat.

"It is the custom," Black Cat said, "to bring our best horses into our lodges at night, or the Sioux would steal them."

Captain Lewis did not need to be warned of the Teton Sioux. Yet, after all his precautions, the Sioux almost killed four of his hunters. The men went out with a sled, made by the Corps's carpenters, to bring in a cache of meat. About a hundred Sioux warriors attacked them twenty miles below the fort and got away with four of their horses.

Lewis called for twenty volunteers from his Corps to go after the thieves, who had also stolen horses from the Lower Mandan Village. Big White, chief of the Lower Village, joined the volunteers, but brought only four of his warriors. His men, he said, did not like to go to battle in below-zero weather. They would punish the Sioux in the spring.

Taking two dogsleds filled with equipment, Lewis and his men trailed the Sioux on foot for thirty miles, then camped for the night. The next day they came to one of their own hunting shacks, which the Corps had built on the prairie. The Sioux had stolen the Corps's cache of meat and burned the shack.

Lewis said the raiders must be punished or they would continue to steal the Corps's food and horses. He and his posse stayed on the trail of the raiders for a week, but never caught the Sioux on their stolen horses.

Since Lewis was not going back empty-handed, he turned to hunting. He sent his men out in a wide circle to close in and drive game toward the center. The volunteers returned to the fort with fourteen elk and thirty-six deer on the two dogsleds. The meat was very welcome at the fort and at the Mandan villages, where Lewis shared it.

It was troubling to Lewis that the raiders had escaped without punishment. Danger from the Tetons was his main reason for having kept the keelboat and Corporal Warfington's soldiers at the fort over the winter. He had planned to send them back to St. Louis at once, but now decided that the keelboat should wait until spring. Then it could pass the Teton villages with less risk while the warriors were on buffalo hunts.

Chief Big White liked to visit the fort. He had been west as far as the mouth of the Yellowstone River, where it entered the Missouri. He felt important discussing with the two captains what lay ahead of them. He instructed Clark, who was drawing a map by putting together all the information he and Lewis had gained from questioning trappers, traders, and Indian hunters.

Squatting in the compound, Big White drew on the ground with a stick. "Here the river goes," he said. "I do not know how far. And here the mountains." The chief took damp earth in his hands and squeezed clumps of the clay, which he set down for mountains.

Lewis urged Big White to go, in the spring, to visit Jefferson. He wanted at least one chief to accept the President's invitation. He repeated Jefferson's promise, "You will go in safety. Soldiers will guard the keelboat. And we will return you safely to your village again."

Big White shook his head. "Maybe I go with *you*, if you come back from the Shining Mountains." He meant the Rockies.

Captain Lewis had to be content with Big White's promise, although privately he hoped that Jefferson would send a ship to the West Coast to pick up the Corps of Discovery. The President had talked about doing this, if it were possible, to save the men a long, hard return trip.

On the eleventh of February, a new member was added to the Corps of Discovery. The interpreter, Charbonneau, came to Lewis in agitation. He said that his wife, Sacajawea, needed medicine as she was having her first baby. Lewis considered Charbonneau something of a coward, but Sacajawea was only sixteen years old and far from her own people. She was a Shoshone Indian stolen four years ago from her home in the mountains by an enemy raiding party. Charbonneau had bought her from her Indian captors for his wife.

Lewis went to the barracks where the interpreter lived. Jusseaume, Big White's French interpreter-trader, was with Sacajawea. A squaw, Otter Woman, stood by helplessly.

Lewis had taken care of his men in illness or accident. He had treated the infections and sickness of the Mandans who came to him. He did not know what to do for Sacajawea. Jusseaume, who was married to an Indian, said that the Mandans gave their squaws crushed rattlesnake tails to ease birth.

Lewis had several rattles from snakes. He had planned to send them to Jefferson. He got a rattler's tail and crushed two rings of it between his fingers into a half cup of water. He handed it to Jusseaume, who helped Sacajawea drink. In a short time her son was born and named Jean Baptiste.

. Sacajawea carried the baby everywhere on her back, no matter what work she was doing around the fort. The men liked to stop and speak to the baby and give him tastes of sugar, which he licked from their fingers. Captain Clark was particularly fond of the little brown-skinned baby. High above his own shock of red hair he often swung the baby in play. He called Baptiste "Pomp," a pet name for babies in Kentucky.

The Mandan Indians showed their liking for the two captains by calling them nicknames too. Clark was Captain Red. Lewis was Captain Long Knife, for the sword he often wore.

Late in February the men were finally able to cut the keelboat and the two pirogues from the ice of the Missouri, which had piled up, almost covering them. Although the weather remained cold, Lewis thought the willows had begun to change color. Their bark was yellow-green. Spring was coming.

While Captain Clark and the French rivermen were making dugout canoes from large cottonwood trees, Lewis carefully labeled and packed specimens of prairie life to send to President Jefferson. The keelboat, now emptied of the Corps's equipment, could carry back the boxes to St. Louis. Everything he sent would be new to the East. How delighted Jefferson would be with the dried herbs and plants, Wilson with the new species of birds!

Among the items in his boxes were skeletons or hides of the antelope, black-tailed deer, mule deer, wolf, buffalo, white weasel, marten, prairie hare (jackrabbit), horns of the mountain ram. He packed one tin box of new insects and mice, one with specimens of soil that might contain minerals or ore.

Another box held earthen dishes and tools used by the Indians. Plants and tuberous roots that the Mandans ate for food or used as medicine were also packed.

Lewis had the carpenters make three wooden cages in which he sent home alive a pair of burrowing squirrels (prairie dogs), four magpies, and a prairie hen.

Late in March, Lewis joyfully told Clark that he had seen a flock of wild geese and another of wild swan. They were flying toward the north. A few days later the ice in the river broke up in a sudden thaw. The Mandans set fire to the prairie to bring in their hunters from all sides. Lewis watched the Indians jump from one cake of ice to the other as they roped the buffalo that tried to cross the river, but fell through the ice and floated helplessly in the numbing water.

Lewis gave his men a few days off to amuse themselves with dancing and visiting the Indians, while he wrote last-minute letters to go on the keelboat. As soon as the ice melted enough, the expedition would start west again.

He wrote a long letter to his mother, telling her about the beautiful prairie country through which he had passed. "One of the fairest portions of the globe," he wrote, "nor do I believe that there is in the universe a similar extent of country equally fertile, well-watered, and intersected with such a number of navigable streams."

He wanted her to know that his long absence and the risks were well worth his taking. He asked her not to worry about him. Every member of his party was trustworthy. He was in good health and good spirits and should be home in about a year and a half.

"You may expect me in Albermarle about the last of September [1806]. I only regret that I cannot have the pleasure of seeing you as often as I did while I was in Washington."

In his letter to Jefferson, Lewis apologized for not sending the keelboat back sooner. He said he realized that the President may have worried when the boat did not return in the fall as planned. But the delay had proved necessary due to the trouble with the Sioux and an early winter. It had also given him time to collect and package the specimens he was sending in the boxes. Captain Clark was sending his notes, scribbled and unsorted, but a fair record of his observations to this point in their journey.

Lewis wrote that he would keep his own notes. He hoped to have time next winter to set them in better order for the many government officials and scientists interested in the different subjects he had observed.

He ended his letter: "I shall set out on my voyage in the course of a few days and feel the most perfect confidence that we shall reach the Pacific Ocean this summer. The party are now in health and perfect spirits, attached to the enterprise and anxious to proceed; not a whisper of discontent or murmur is to be heard among them. With such men, I feel every confidence necessary to insure success. The party, with Captain Clark and myself, consists of thirty-one white persons, one Negro man, and two Indians."

The permanent party were the two captains and York. Sergeants: John Ordway, Nathaniel Pryor, Patrick Gass. Privates: William Bratton, John Collins, John Colter, Peter Cruzatte, Joseph Fields, Reuben Fields, Robert Frazier, George Gibson, Silas Goodrich, Hugh Hall, Thomas P. Howard, Francis Labiche, Baptiste Lepage, Hugh McNeal, John Potts, George Shannon, John Shields, John B. Thompson, William Werner, Joseph Whitehouse, Richard Windsor, Peter Wiser. Two interpreters: George Drouillard and Touissant Charbonneau with his wife, Sacajawea, and their baby son.

At Fort Mandan, Lewis had prepared for the journey west as carefully as he had before leaving St. Louis. Yet there was a difference. From Mandan on, little was known about what lay ahead. The Indians told him that the Missouri River finally led to a great falls, beyond which was the gate of the mountains, where no Indian canoes had gone.

Sacajawea told Lewis that her people, the Shoshones, lived in the mountains and had many horses, which they prized highly. They could not travel the swift mountain streams in canoes as the Missouri River Indians did.

Lewis knew he must be able to buy horses when the expedition could no longer use boats. He had managed friendly relations with every tribe except the Tetons. He believed he could trade with the Shoshones.

On April 7, 1805, Mandans lined the banks of the river to see the men of Fort Mandan off. Captain Lewis and his Corps of Discovery waved good-by to the keelboat's crew of nine and a small canoe that carried two French hunters and followed the armed keelboat. Lewis had sent the hunters to provide meat for the crew on its return trip to St. Louis.

Then the Corps of Discovery turned to their own boats, which were packed and ready to move west. The "fleet" was the two large pirogues with sails plus men at the oars, and six small dug-out canoes made during the winter.

Clark led with the red pirogue and its crew.

The white pirogue, stronger built than the red, carried all the important papers in oil-skin packets, the gifts for the Indians, medicines, and extra ammunition. One-eyed Peter Cruzatte was captain of the white pirogue with a crew of three men. Charbonneau, Sacajawea, and Pomp were also on board.

Lewis, eager to be started, walked along the bank of the river ahead of the boats with his dog, Scammon. That night he wrote in his journal:

"We are now about to penetrate a country at least two thousand miles in width, on which the foot of civilized man has never trodden; the good or evil it has in store for us is yet to be determined, and these little vessels contain every article by which we can expect to subsist or defend ourselves. . . . The picture which now presents itself to me is a most pleasing one, entertaining as I do the most confident hope of succeeding in a voyage which had formed a darling project of mine for the last ten years. I could but esteem this moment of departure as among the most happy of my life."

6
We Must Have Horses

TWO MONTHS after leaving Fort Mandan, the expedition was stopped while Lewis and Clark decided which of two forks in the river to follow. No one, Indian or trapper, had told them that they would come to a junction of two wide, fast-flowing rivers. Which fork came through the Rocky Mountains?

"The Indians told us we would come to great falls in the river which our boats could not traverse," Clark said as he and Lewis stood on the bank and studied the two rivers. "They never mentioned this fork."

"It's truly an unknown land," Lewis said, "and we cannot afford to make a mistake. If we take the wrong fork and lose time, we may not get over the mountains before winter."

"The north fork is deeper," Clark said. "Its water flows in the same boiling, rolling manner as the Missouri we have covered, and its color is the same thick, whitish brown."

The listening men nodded. They thought the north fork looked more like the Missouri.

"But," Lewis said, "the south fork is swift and clear. I've seen the same kind of flat, smooth stones on the bottom of mountain streams at home. Such clear, fast water is more likely to come from the falls in high country than the muddy water is."

"You're right about that," Clark said.

Lewis said, "There's only one way to be sure. Tomorrow you lead a party of men up the south fork. I'll explore the north fork, only a march of a day or two. If one of us finds the falls, we'll know which river is the Missouri."

That evening beside the campfire, Lewis cleaned his rifle. He hoped to find deer or buffalo on his trip upriver, so the Corps could eat fresh meat. He needed the rifle in perfect condition to protect himself too. Recently the expedition had entered grizzly bear country, which the Indians had warned them about. Two of the Corps's best hunters had barely escaped with their lives when a grizzly chased them.

Lewis looked at his men as they sewed reinforcements of buffalo hide on the soles of their worn moccasins. Their feet were bruised, bleeding, and infected where rocks had cut them. Clark was pulling thorns of prickly pear cactus from his feet. Yet not one man complained about his pain or the incredibly hard work of pulling the pirogues' towropes while wading waist-deep through icy water. Lewis had never been prouder of his volunteer Corps of Discovery.

He must get them through the mountains in safety. The river current was already too fast for the boats. He must find the Shoshone Indians and horses soon.

He wondered if he should talk again to Sacajawea. She was very ill and lying in a tent, where Clark had given her medicine. Lewis decided not to disturb her. She had already told him that she knew nothing about the country through which they were passing. He hoped she would recognize her own Shoshone country when they reached it.

The young Indian woman had proved herself a valuable member of the expedition. From the first, she had hunted edible roots for the hungry men. Like the Arikaras, Sacajawea dug in the ground with a stick and gathered the wild beans that mice had collected and hidden for winter.

And she had kept her head when a storm hit the white pirogue and turned it over, spilling some of its valuable cargo into the river. Cruzatte, fighting to tighten the sail's brace, had shouted to Charbonneau to grab the helm and help right the pirogue. The terrified interpreter had frozen in fear and fallen on his knees to pray. From the riverbank, Lewis too shouted at Charbonneau. Seeing that he was about to lose the precious journals, medicines, ammunition, and presents for the Indians, Lewis threw down his gun to leap into the river and swim after the floating packets.

Ahead, Clark shouted at him to stop. Lewis paused. The swift current was icy cold. He would drown in such water before he could cover the three hundred yards to the pirogue. Yet he would rather risk his life than lose the journals and supplies.

Then he saw Cruzatte threaten Charbonneau with his gun, so that the frightened man did his part. The pirogue was righted. Sacajawea had leaned far into the water and caught up most of the packages that had been washed overboard.

Early in the morning the two leaders and their parties set off up the two forks of the river. When Lewis shouldered his pack and

took up his gun, Scammon limped on three legs, barking and pleading to go along.

Lewis rubbed the thick mat of hair between his dog's black ears. "Not this time," he said.

Scammon had been a real hunter. He had chased swimming squirrels and wild fowl and caught them in the water when the men needed food the most. The big dog had even brought in an antelope in this way. But he had recently tackled a beaver in the water.

The beaver's sharp teeth had cut through one of Scammon's leg bones, severing an artery. Lewis had worked with him far into the night, sure that his dog would die. Scammon was recovering now, but Lewis would not let him undertake a long, dangerous march to discover the right fork to follow.

After a day's travel, Lewis felt sure that the north fork came from the north rather than from the west, his route to the Pacific. He named the fork Maria's after one of his cousins. When he returned to camp, he found that Clark, too, had decided that the south fork was the Missouri, although neither party had found the falls.

The men decided to cache the red pirogue, which was too heavy and large to be pulled up the swift mountain water. They drew the pirogue onto a small island in the middle of Maria's River, tied it to a tree, and covered it with bushes. If they had to return overland the next year, they could use the pirogue on the way home.

Lewis and four men walked on ahead of Clark and the boats. He told his friend that they would meet at the falls. That night Lewis was so sick with fever and stomach cramps that he could not eat or walk. He had no medicine with him, so he asked Joseph Fields to gather chokecherry twigs, boil them in water, and make a strong tea. Lewis drank the bitter medicinal tea at night and again in the morning.

Although weak, Lewis was determined to go on. He sent the men by different paths to hunt for meat. Alone on the third day of climbing into high country, he heard ahead a roaring like the sound of falling water. He climbed on a rock and saw what might be a column of smoke rising into the sky. It disappeared, then returned. He knew it must be spray from giant falls.

Filled with joy and excitement, he scrambled on. The roaring grew louder, finally too tremendous to be mistaken for anything but the Great Falls of the Missouri.

He climbed up a chain of rocks, about twenty feet high, opposite the center of the falls. Perpendicular cliffs of rock left only a narrow passage, which squeezed the water into a cascade of incredible swiftness. And this cascade was not all of the falls.

"The remaining part of about 200 yards, a smooth even sheet of water falling over a precipice of at least eighty feet, on my right, forms the grandest sight I ever beheld," he wrote that night in his journal. "Projecting rocks below receive the water in its

passage down and break it into a perfect white foam which as-
sumes a thousand forms in a moment, sometimes flying up into
jets of sparkling foam to the height of fifteen or twenty feet, and
are scarcely formed before large rolling bodies of the same beaten
and foaming water is thrown over and conceals them."

Below the falls were a few acres of beautiful bottom land with
cottonwood and cedar trees. Here was the place to camp and
prepare to portage around the falls.

The next day Lewis sent one of his men back to meet Clark
and tell him that they had chosen correctly. This *was* the Missouri.

Then Lewis went out to hunt buffalo. He wanted a large supply of meat for the men, and to dry and carry into the mountains.
He knew that buffalo could not roam much higher than the
plains below the falls.

In the afternoon Lewis came upon a herd of about a thousand
buffalo. He shot one. Before he could reload his single-shot rifle,
he heard something behind him. He turned to see a great grizzly
bear almost upon him.

He wrote in his journal later: "In the first moment, I drew up
my gun to shoot, but at the same instance recollected that it was
not loaded and that he was too near for me to hope to perform
that operation before he reached me, as he was then briskly advancing on me. It was an open level plain, not a bush within a
mile or a tree within 300 yards of me. The riverbank was sloping
and not more than three feet above the water. In short, there was
no place by means of which I could conceal myself from this
monster until I could charge my rifle. In this situation I thought
of retreating in a brisk walk as fast as he was advancing until I
could reach a tree about 300 yards below me, but I had no sooner
turned myself about but he pitched at me, open-mouthed, and at
full speed. I ran about eighty yards and found he gained on me

fast. I then ran into the water to such depth that I could stand and he would be obliged to swim. In water about waist deep, I turned and presented the point of my espontoon. At this instant he arrived at the edge of the water. The moment I put myself into this attitude of defense, he suddenly wheeled about, as if frightened, declined to combat on such unequal grounds, and retreated.

"As soon as I saw him run in that manner, I returned to the shore and charged my gun, which I still had retained in my hand throughout this curious adventure. I saw him run through the level open field about three miles, until he disappeared into the woods. During the whole distance he ran at full speed, sometimes appearing to look behind him as if he expected pursuit.

"On examination I saw the ground torn by his great talons, and felt a little gratified that he had declined the combat. My gun reloaded, I felt confidence once more in my strength."

Lewis had planned to stay out all night, sleeping on the ground. He had scarcely escaped the grizzly, when he came upon a mountain lion "which couched itself down like a cat looking as if it designed to spring upon me. I took aim at it and fired. It instantly disappeared into its den."

He walked on three hundred yards when three bull buffalo, probably protecting their herd, ran full speed at him.

"I did not choose," he wrote, "to remain all night at that place."

He made his way back to camp after dark, his feet pierced with prickly pear cactus on the way. When he awoke the next morning, a rattlesnake hung in a tree just over his head. He killed it with one shot.

After so many narrow escapes in one day and night, he wondered if he might not live a charmed life. At least my work in this world is not finished, he thought.

In a few days Clark and the boats reached the falls. The expedition camped and prepared to haul all its goods around the Great Falls, a distance of almost twenty miles. They cached the white pirogue for their return trip. They transferred their valuable baggage into two rough carts, which they made. The solid wooden wheels were formed by cutting across the trunk of the largest cottonwood tree they could find, twenty-two inches in diameter. They made the axles of tougher willow trees.

After three weeks of strenuous labor in preparation, the expedition began the portage. The men hauled the carts and their dugout canoes with all their strength, often pulling themselves and their loads up with one hand while catching hold of rocks or tufts of coarse grass with the other. They moved only a short distance each day.

Storms came in the afternoons, almost blowing them off the high places, chilling them with hail and rain. Mosquitoes bit them. Swarms of gnats swam in their eyes so they seemed to be constantly weeping.

"But," Lewis wrote, "no man complains. All go on cheerfully."

The clothing the men had worn from St. Louis had given out.

Lewis and Clark, like their men, were dressed in shirts and breeches of elk skin now. With toughened, browned skins, they all looked like Indians.

On July 15 they once again put their eight small dugouts in the river. The canoes were heavy-laden with dried meat, grease, the journals, and gifts for the Indians. Lewis continued to scout ahead of the boats, and to hunt and help keep the men supplied with meat.

The river soon entered the mountains. Here the Missouri flowed through a long, steep canyon with cliffs so high and perpendicular that the men were forced to wade in the edge of the foaming water over slippery rocks and pull the canoes. On July 25 they came to three forks in the Missouri.

Lewis and Clark studied the three rivers, all of them much the same size, all swift and difficult. They decided that these three rivers were the beginning of the Missouri, which they calculated to be 2,464 miles in length from its mouth at St. Louis.

Clark said that the north fork was his choice to ascend. It had the greatest flow of water and seemed to lead most directly into the western mountains, which they had to cross. Lewis agreed with him. They named the north fork, which they followed, the Jefferson River.

Finally on August 8, Sacajawea called, "Beaver Head. Beaver Head." She had recognized the point of a high plain resembling a beaver's head. Joyfully she told Lewis that her people, the Shoshones, lived in villages on a river beyond a mountain that ran to the west, not too far distant. There was a pass, she said, where her people crossed the Bitterroot Mountains.

That night Lewis wrote in his journal: "I determined to proceed tomorrow with a small party down the river until I find the Indians who have horses, if it should cost me the trip of a month, for without horses we will be obliged to leave a great part of our

stores, of which, it appears to me, we have already a stock sufficiently small for the length of the voyage before us."

Lewis tramped for three days with Drouillard, Shields, and
McNeal. They thought they saw smoke from Indian campfires,
but the Indians always disappeared before the men reached
them. Lewis was so anxious to find Indians that he sent Drouillard and Shields another way to search.

Suddenly Lewis and McNeal saw, far ahead, an Indian on
horseback. Lewis watched him through his spyglass. The young
brave rode bareback on a beautiful horse.

"He could lead us to his tribe," Lewis told McNeal, "if only he
will let me approach him and show that we are friendly."

Lewis walked to meet the Indian, careful not to frighten him.
The Indian saw him and halted. Lewis took a blanket from his
pack and lifted it above his head, then brought it down in a
spreading motion upon the ground, the Indian invitation of
friendship or "talk."

The young Indian waited, watchful. Lewis took gifts from his
pack and spread them on the blanket. He handed his gun to
McNeal and went forward unarmed to meet the strange Indian.

He might have succeeded, but Drouillard and Shields came
around a hill. The Indian turned his horse in alarm and galloped
away.

Lewis and his men followed the horse's tracks until an afternoon shower erased them. That night they camped beside a
small valley stream and built such a big fire that it could be seen
for miles. No Indian came to talk.

In the morning they walked and climbed until they came upon
an Indian trail, which they followed as it wound high among the
peaks. Lewis was sure this must be the Indian passage over the
Continental Divide.

The men finally stood on the dividing ridge and discovered im-

mense ranges of snow-covered mountains still to the west. This
was disappointing. Lewis had hoped to find the Columbia River
beginning on the westward slopes.

Going down the western slope, the road seemed much steeper.
After walking about five miles, the men came into a little valley
and surprised an Indian man with two women and a dog. Lewis
held up the American flag. He called out the Shoshone word for
white man, *"Tab-ba-bone, tab-ba-bone,"* but the Indians fled.

Lewis and his men followed again. They came around some
bushes, face to face with two Indian girls and an old woman.
The Indians were too close to run. They went down upon the
ground and bent their heads as if they expected to be killed.

Captain Lewis took the woman's hands and lifted her. He
pulled up his shirt sleeve and showed her his skin, saying, *"Tab-
ba-bone."* Then he gave the woman and girls some beads and a
pewter looking-glass.

By sign language Drouillard repeated Lewis's words, "We
come in peace. We are anxious to meet and make friends with
the chiefs and warriors of your nation."

They had walked about two miles with the women, when a
party of sixty warriors galloped toward Lewis at full speed. Suddenly they halted. Lewis handed his gun to his men and walked
forward carrying the American flag.

It was a touchy moment. The Indian women ran toward their
men and showed them the presents Lewis had given them. The
young chief dismounted and came forward to meet Lewis with
two of his warriors.

"Chief Cameahwait," he stated his name. He gave the captain
a hug of welcome, pressing his painted cheek against Lewis's face
and saying, *"Ah-hi-e, ah-hi-e."*

Lewis and his men were taken to a Shoshone village, where
about one hundred men and three hundred women and children

lived in cone-shaped lodges made of willow boughs. The chief said there were a number of such villages at a distance.

Lewis sat with the Indians on a circle of antelope skins and went through a long ceremony of smoking the pipe. The women and children were allowed to stand nearby and watch, for these were the first white men they had ever seen.

When Lewis's turn came to speak, he presented gifts of blue beads and red face paint, which he knew the Indians of every tribe prized. He gave them an American flag and told them the reason for his journey, and how much he needed horses and guides who knew the mountain trails.

Chief Cameahwait asked an older man to speak to Lewis. This Indian, Toby, had been a prisoner of the Nez Percé tribes who lived on the Clearwater River above the Columbia River.

Toby shook his head. "Not go through the high mountains," he warned. "Men try. Men die."

Lewis looked at the fine horses grazing near the camp and saw a horse staked at every lodge, ready to be ridden at a moment's notice.

"Someone must get through the mountains," he said. "These are not ordinary horses. Many wear Spanish brands. You must trade with the Spaniards. I will trade you whatever you wish for thirty horses."

The Indians looked at one another, but made no promise.

Chief Cameahwait said, "We traded furs for the horses with the Spanish below the Yellowstone River. But they will not trade us guns to hunt. We need guns, for my people are hungry."

"American traders will supply you with guns to hunt," Lewis promised. "First I must cross the mountains and reach the western sea."

Toby said that the Nez Percés had told him of a great river that runs toward the setting sun and finally is lost in a great lake of water that tastes and smells bad.

Lewis was sure that he meant the Columbia River, which flowed into the Pacific Ocean. He urged Toby to tell him how to get there.

Toby said that a Nez Percé hunting party had returned him to his tribe. They had followed an old buffalo trail, unmarked through boulders, ice, and brush. It took many days across the snowy mountains, and many more days over a sandy desert where no food or water could be found. All of this country was very cold. There was no timber for fires.

The circle of warriors looked at Lewis as if enough had been said. Only a very foolish man would undertake such a journey.

It was late in the evening. No one had eaten all day. Indian

women brought a wooden platter of cakes made from pressed berries dried in the sun.

"It is all we have to eat," Chief Cameahwait said. "Game is scarce. We tried to go down on the Missouri River plains to hunt buffalo before winter sets in. Enemy tribes of Blackfeet and Minnetarees attacked us. We lost twenty men and many horses."

Lewis saw that the Indians were lean and hungry. With bows and arrows they could not bring in enough meat to feed their families.

The next morning Lewis sent his three men to hunt for meat. He remained in camp to bargain for horses. And with gifts and promises, he persuaded Toby and his son to go with the expedition as guides. Toby said that he remembered little of the way. Lewis answered that Toby knew more about the mountains than strangers could.

Scarcely had Lewis made his bargain with Toby, when an Indian who had followed the hunters ran home crying that Drouillard had shot a deer. In an instant every warrior was on his horse, whipping it to reach the hunter.

Lewis rode with them. He saw the Indians tumble from their horses and grab the intestines of the deer, which Drouillard was dressing. The men tore and ate the raw meat like a pack of famished dogs.

Later Lewis wrote: "I viewed these poor starved devils with pity and compassion. I directed McNeal to skin the deer and reserve one quarter for us, the balance I gave to the Chief to divide among his people; they devoured the whole of it without cooking."

Then Lewis told his men to bring in all the meat they could for the Indians. They brought two more deer and an antelope. The Indians held a feast and danced with joy far into the night.

Again Lewis tried to trade for horses. He said that his friend,

Captain Clark, was coming up the river with boats and trading goods to pay for the horses. "Come with me and meet him?" he said.

The chief agreed. Many of the warriors shook their heads. The chief changed his mind, saying that his warriors believed this might be a trap. Lewis might be in the pay of their enemy tribes who would be waiting in ambush at the river.

Knowing how proud the Indians were, Lewis said, "I am sorry you do not trust us, for if no Americans come here to trade, you will never have guns or ammunition. I hope there are some among you who are not afraid to die. If so, let them come with me and see for themselves that I am telling the truth."

Chief Cameahwait leaped upon his horse. Some of his warriors followed and went to meet Clark's boats with Lewis. In a camp on the shore of the river, the ceremony of the pipe was held again, this time with both leaders of the expedition.

Seated on a white robe, six small pearl-like shells tied in his long black hair, the young chief received his guests. Every man removed his moccasins when he sat down, a sign that he would walk barefoot forever if he failed to tell the truth here. When the pipe had been passed, Lewis spoke again of the strength and friendship of the United States, which he represented. He repeated his reasons for crossing the mountains.

"We must have horses," he said. "We will pay you well."

The chief thanked the white men for their friendship. He wanted trade with their great nation. He could not spare enough horses, at present, to carry their baggage over the mountain. His people were hungry. They must ride their best horses to hunt for buffalo again before winter.

However, he added, he would give the white men several of his own horses. He hoped they could trade with other Shoshone villages for the remainder they had to have.

Lewis could not blame the chief. He wanted to ask him where to find other Indians to get the horses he needed. Knowing the limits of Drouillard's sign language and Charbonneau's understanding of the Shoshone tongue, Lewis sent for Sacajawea to translate more exactly.

When the young Indian woman saw Cameahwait, she ran forward and embraced him, weeping. He pushed her away in surprise. Then even Lewis understood her cries, "Brother, my brother."

The men soon understood that this was the village of the Shoshones from whom Sacajawea had been stolen as a girl. Since that time, her brother had become a chief. He was pleased to see her, but he did not change his mind about the number of horses he could spare.

That evening the two captains talked together in their tent. Clark said that he would take a few men and explore ahead a distance. Perhaps he could find a river that would lead them to the Columbia. Lewis could continue to bargain for more horses.

"If any Indian has crossed those mountains," Lewis said as he spread a buffalo robe on the ground for his bed, "we can do it."

The tall redhead looked at his determined friend and smiled. "I reckon we have to," he said.

7
Fort Clatsop

"WHAT'S the most important thing to set down?" Clark asked Lewis as they wrote in their journals the experiences of the past four months. From the day the Corps of Discovery had left the Shoshone village with their baggage on twenty-nine poor pack horses, until this New Year's Day, 1806, the captains had scarcely had time or strength to write more than a few notes. Now they sat across from each other at a big tree-stump table in Fort Clatsop, built much like Fort Mandan. They were taking advantage of the continuous rain on the Pacific Coast to set their records straight.

"That we survived," Lewis answered.

It was true. No words could describe the more than two hundred miles they had portaged over the mountains. Their hunger. The cold. Brush so thick they could scarcely push their way. Then only wind and boulders where the old Nez Percé buffalo trail followed the ridges rather than the valleys. They were forced to travel on rocky cliffs or ledges so narrow that several horses bearing baggage had tumbled into deep canyons below.

After that, Lewis had packed his journals on his back, for he feared their loss more than his own life. His journals carried the

proof that Americans had come this way, and they strengthened
his country's claim to the Far West.

He bent to his writing now. He described the Nez Percés and
the Flathead Indians as some of the best red men they met. They
had little more than salmon and camas roots to eat, but they had
shared these with the Corps. How sick all the men had been from
eating camas root after going so long without food!

"Our situation was desperate when we came among them,"
Lewis wrote. "Our horses and men alike were sick and weak
from want of food. The Nez Percés helped us make dugout
canoes from great pine trees which grow there. By portaging
many times, we could go from the rivers Clearwater, to the
Snake, to the Columbia. Chief Twisted Hair agreed to keep our
horses, which we branded, until we returned next spring."

The men had welcomed boats again after almost two months
on "the worst road ever traveled by man." Friendly Nez Percés
guides had brought them to the village of the Walla Walla Indians, and to their first sight of the dangerous rapids and falls of the
Columbia River. Everything in this country was bigger and
wilder than anything they had ever seen before: the trees, the
rocky cliffs, the raging white waters.

Squeezed between cliffs with no banks on which to land, the
men had little hope of passing safely. Somehow, Cruzatte, who
was as excellent with boats as he was with a fiddle, had piloted
them through, with only the loss of two dugouts in the four weeks
down the river.

Lewis remembered how disappointed the watching Chinook
Indians had been when the white men handled their canoes so
well. These mid-Columbia tribes had hoped for wrecks to sal-
vage. The Chinooks were a thieving lot. The Corps had to watch
every moment or their food and tools would be stolen. They
even tried to steal Scammon.

Once the Chinooks took rifles from two men while they slept.

Lewis led his men into the Chinook camp and demanded the rifles. Although they were greatly outnumbered, Lewis ordered his men not to shoot. No Indian had been harmed on the entire trip. They would get the guns without killing anyone now, he said.

Sullenly the Chinooks gave up the rifles, perhaps because the Corps showed no fear. Perhaps, too, they did not know of Lewis's order not to shoot.

At first the expedition had camped near the seashore while they looked for a place to winter. Lewis wanted to remain as close to the Pacific as possible to keep watch for a passing ship. He carried President Jefferson's letter of credit, which promised that the Treasury of the United States would honor any bill presented by Captain Lewis for the return of his men and baggage by ship.

Lewis knew a ship occasionally stopped there, for the Clatsop Indians spoke sailor-English—"rascal, heave the lead, musket, powder, knife."

Clark would have preferred to winter a few miles back up the Columbia River. He disliked the sound of the surf.

"It roars in front of our tents like repeated rolls of thunder," he had said to Lewis, "and has roared that way every day since we arrived in sight of this great western ocean. But I'll vote along with you. We should build near enough to see ships."

After exploring for sites, Lewis called the members of the expedition together and offered two possible places to build the fort. He asked every member to vote, including York and Sacajawea.

Now as he wrote in his journal, he thought that the vote to build Fort Clatsop south of the Columbia River and inland a little way, was probably the first time a black man, or any woman, had voted on a United States' decision.

A long monotonous winter began. It rained almost every day,

and the men had little to do after the fort was completed. To keep them from being idle, Lewis permitted them to play quoits and to run races with the Clatsop Indians, to fiddle and dance as usual. Few Indians were allowed to enter the fort as they had at Fort Mandan. The Clatsops, Lewis thought, were not as bad as the Chinooks, but the Pacific Indians could not compare in honesty, trustworthiness, and friendly hospitality with the Mandans, Nez Percés, and Shoshones.

Food was a problem. "If there is any game, our hunters can bring it in," Lewis wrote. But meat would not keep in the rainy climate. It even spoiled in the smokehouse Lewis had the men build. They gorged themselves on antelope when they had it. Between hunts they tried blubber from a whale stranded on the beach, beaver and otter meat, fish, even dog meat, which they bought from the Clatsop Indians.

No ship came. Lewis began to prepare for their return by the way they had come. He had almost no trading goods left and was forced to give his own best, lace-trimmed uniform coat to the Clatsop Chief Comowool for a canoe.

Anxious as everyone was to leave for home, Lewis warned the men that it would be folly to attempt the open plains before April. "We know there is no fuel except a few small dry shrubs," he said, "and the Indians have told us that snow lies as deep as twenty feet over miles of mountain pass until late spring."

In spite of all they had endured in coming over the pass, the expedition decided to leave a week earlier than April. In case anything should happen to them on the way home, Lewis drew up a document that he left with Chief Comowool with whom he had become friendly.

He asked the chief to keep the paper until a ship came, then send it, by the ship's captain, to the President of the United States. He told the chief that it was a most important paper.

It was. Lewis had several copies made. He nailed one on the wall of his room in the fort, along with a map Clark had drawn of the route they had covered. With these papers, Lewis knew that the U.S. Government could claim the territory over which he had passed, even if he failed to reach home.

He listed the names of every man in his Corps and wrote: "The object of the list is that, through the medium of some civilized person who may see the same, it may be made known to the informed world that the party consisting of the persons whose names are hereunto annexed, and who were sent out by the Government of the U'States in May 1804 to explore the interior of the continent of North America, did penetrate the same by way of the Missouri and Columbia Rivers, to the discharge of the latter into the Pacific Ocean, where they arrived on the 14th of November 1805, and whence they departed the 23d day of March 1806 on their return to the United States by the same route they had come out."

8
Two Years, Four Months, and Ten Days

SEVERAL TIMES during the long difficult journey back to Fort Mandan, Lewis had reason to believe that the notice he left at Fort Clatsop might be the only thing left of the expedition. The Corps reached the mountains when the snow was still so deep that they could not go on for five weeks. The men ate bark, roots, and seeds from pinecones. All of them were sick and might have died of starvation if the Nez Percés had not taken pity on them and given them horses to eat.

It was the middle of June before the men began a second climb over the slippery snow-covered ledges of the pass. With sixty-six horses and five Nez Percé guides, the expedition finally reached the Bitterroot Valley, an eight-hundred-mile trip that had cost them three months' time. Here they rested for two days and repaired their guns and dried their packs.

Lewis and Clark held one of their planning sessions. They felt that the worst was behind them. They would split the Corps into several parts so that each could explore a different area and carry home more information.

Clark, with most of the men, would march to the Yellowstone River, hollow out canoes, and go down the Yellowstone to the

Missouri River. Sergeant Ordway with nine men would go down the Jefferson River to the Great Falls of the Missouri, where they had cached the white pirogue. He would bring the pirogue and canoes to meet Lewis at the fork of the Marias River. Lewis planned to cut across country horseback to explore the Marias from the north down to the Missouri.

Lewis, Drouillard, and the two Fields brothers had ridden only a few days toward the Marias, when their Nez Percé guides said they must return to their tribes. Lewis tried to persuade the friendly, goodhearted Nez Percés to go with him. They refused to go into Blackfoot Indian country, which Lewis was about to enter.

"Blackfeet very bad warriors," his guides said. "They steal your horses and kill you."

Lewis smoked a last pipe of peace with his Nez Percé friends, gave them one of his shirts, some handkerchiefs, and divided his small store of powder with them. The next morning he set out without guides.

Drouillard came upon a wounded buffalo. He examined the arrows in it. Blackfeet. Now Lewis and his three men were extra watchful by day and by night. They explored north on the Marias and were on their return to the Missouri, when Lewis saw many Indians on horses on a hilltop. Looking through his spyglass, Lewis saw that the Indians were watching Drouillard, who was hunting alone some distance from camp.

They seemed about to attack the hunter. Lewis told Joseph Fields to lift the American flag to catch the attention of the Indians. Alone, Captain Lewis advanced slowly toward the warriors. He held out his hand palm up in the sign of peace. An Indian warrior galloped straight at him, followed by the others.

Lewis had learned a little of the universal Indian sign language. He said he wanted to talk to them.

They allowed Drouillard and the Fields brothers to approach. Through the interpreter, Lewis asked the Indians to go to their village and bring back their chief with other warriors for a council to be held at the fork of the Marias and Missouri Rivers. He said he had friends waiting there.

He could not tell whether the warriors believed he had other men or not. He gave each of them a medal and tobacco. They appeared to be friendly as they made camp for the night. Lewis and his three men camped nearby, for it seemed better to watch the Blackfeet.

During the night, the Indians fell upon Drouillard while he was on guard and stole his gun. Other Indians ran the white men's horses before them.

In the ensuing struggle to save their lives, Reuben Fields and Lewis each killed an Indian who was about to shoot them. All the Blackfeet fled, but Lewis knew they would return with more of their tribe to take revenge for the death of the two warriors. On foot he and his men roped several of the Indian horses that had escaped from their herd.

"We cannot withstand them," Lewis said as he and the men saddled and bridled the horses. "We must outride them. At the Missouri, we may find Ordway's men."

He gave his final orders: "If attacked on the plain, tie the bridles together. Stand behind the horses. Fight it out to the end."

The four men were off. They did not stop until midafternoon, when they reached the Rose River. They rested the horses an hour and a half and went on again. By evening they could scarcely sit in their saddles, but Lewis gave the horses barely two hours' rest. They rode through the darkness until even Lewis gave up.

From his knowledge of the country, Lewis said they had ridden 120 miles in twenty-four hours. He doubted that the Blackfeet would do that. So they lay down on the ground and slept.

At dawn they saddled their horses and rode again toward the Missouri. Soon they heard rifle shots. They hurried toward the sound and could scarcely believe their good fortune when they saw Ordway's white pirogue and the canoes coming downriver.

They followed along the bank to the island where they had cached the red pirogue a year ago. It was too rotted to use.

All the party continued down the Missouri River toward the rendezvous with Clark at the mouth of the Yellowstone. The boats made as much as seventy miles a day now, for they were traveling *with* the current. The men rejoiced that they were in game country again and had meat to eat.

At one overnight stop, Lewis and Cruzatte went on foot to hunt elk. Lewis shot a buck. Cruzatte wounded another. The one-eyed boatman and hunter had suffered snow-blindness in the mountains and could not see as well as he used to. Lewis helped Cruzatte hunt for the wounded elk. Each man went a different way through the thick growth of willows.

Suddenly Lewis heard a shot and felt a searing pain through his left thigh. The bullet had missed the bone, for he could still stand. He shouted to Cruzatte, "You shot me."

There was no answer. Again he called to his companion and had no response. Cruzatte must hear him, Lewis thought. Perhaps Cruzatte had not accidentally shot him, thinking he was the elk. Perhaps Indians had them both in ambush and Cruzatte dared not answer.

Lewis called loudly for Cruzatte to follow and ran for the boats.

At the river camp, Lewis told the men to come with him. He led them back into the willows to save Cruzatte. Soon his leg became so painful that he could no longer stand. He sent the men on.

When darkness came, the men returned. They had found no Indians. A frightened and embarrassed Cruzatte was with them.

He said that he had not heard Lewis shout.

Lewis said nothing. He knew that Cruzatte had been so horrified at shooting his captain accidentally that he had been unable to face him.

The men helped Lewis into the pirogue, for he was weak from pain and loss of blood. He told them what to bring from his pack, and treated his torn flesh with a poultice of Peruvian bark.

A few days later, on August 12, the entire expedition was united again when the pirogue and canoes caught up with Clark's canoes near the junction of the rivers, Yellowstone and Missouri. Clark was very much concerned when he saw his friend's inflamed wound. He insisted on dressing it morning and night. Lewis bore the pain well, but he placed Captain Clark in full charge of the expedition until he was improved. This meant that Clark would have to council with the Indians they met on their way downriver. He also kept the journals up to date, for Lewis could not sit, or lie, or stand comfortably enough to write.

When they reached the Mandan villages, where the Corps had spent the first winter, the Mandans welcomed them with joy. The Indians said their white brothers had been gone so long that they feared they were dead.

Later Clark reported to Lewis, who was confined to the pirogue, on his trip to the villages. "I met the chief of the Little Village of the Minnetarees," Clark said. "He wept and told me that the Blackfeet had killed his son. The tribes have been warring again while we were gone. I don't think we can persuade a chief to go back with us to Washington."

"We must take at least one chief," Lewis said. "This is important to Jefferson. He wants one of their own chiefs to return and tell the Indians that our friendship is genuine, and that the United States is strong and able to protect them from their enemies if they remain our friends."

"Black Cat won't go," Clark said. "He told me that he wished to visit the Great Father of the United States, but was afraid of the Sioux. A Sioux war party attacked this winter and killed eight of his warriors. He will not go down the Missouri past their villages, for they are bad people and will listen to nothing anyone says."

Lewis sat up too suddenly and groaned, impatient with his helplessness when he had so much he wanted to do.

"Big White promised me last year that he would consider going," Lewis said. "Tell him that he will see many wonderful sights and receive many presents. He will be important in the eyes of his people when he returns to tell his stories around the campfires. Tell him that the United States will return him safely to his own village. Jefferson told me to make this promise. It will be kept faithfully."

Much to Lewis's satisfaction, Big White finally agreed to go with the Corps to St. Louis, then on to Washington, if he could take with him his wife and son, and the interpreter, Jusseaume, with his Indian wife and children.

On the afternoon of August 17, Captain Clark gave an order for the pirogue and the line of canoes to set off for St. Louis. All the Mandans from the Lower Village followed along the river-bank. The women cried and wailed for the loss of their chief. Anxiously Lewis watched Big White's canoes, filled with family and baggage, following behind the white pirogue. The Mandan chief's head was bowed in sorrow at leaving his people. He might yet change his mind.

Lewis felt a little sad himself. His wound was healing and he expected to walk before the expedition reached St. Louis. But it was not easy to say good-by to Sacajawea and little Pomp, who remained with Charbonneau near the Mandans. Clark looked particularly unhappy at leaving the little boy. He had offered to take Pomp into his home and give him an education when the boy was old enough to leave his mother.

Almost daily the expedition met trappers and traders going upriver to begin their winter's work, trading for beaver furs and buffalo hides. How many more men were coming into this Indian country after only two years! Lewis thought.

On the seventeenth of September the expedition met a large boat and hailed the captain, who waved his hat and shouted with pleasure. Lewis was able to go on board with Clark and have supper with their old friend, Captain John McClallan of the U.S. Army.

"Everyone in Washington gave you up for dead," McClallan said, "except Jefferson. The President seemed to think that you could handle any situation. But he is worried. He asked me to inquire for you among the Indians."

"You can see we're not scalped," Clark said, looking at the cup in his hand, "but it's a long time since we tasted port like this."

Captain McClallan looked at Clark's shock of red hair, trimmed irregularly by Lewis. He laughed. "I knew by the color of that hair that you weren't a band of Indians," he said. "Still you don't look like the two gentlemen I first knew from Virginia and Kentucky.

"Tell me, how did you survive an adventure of such length and danger? No one thought you could do it."

"Lewis's expert planning," Clark said.

"Clark's nose for geography and skill in handling the boats," Lewis said.

William Clark leaned forward to emphasize his words. "Planning wasn't all, of course. In emergencies, instinct and intelligence have to work fast together. There's a right time to do, or say, a thing. There aren't many people who have the sense to know that right moment. Lewis does. He handled the Indians

SHE-HE-KE, a Mandan chief called Big White, accompanied the expedition back to Washington. Lewis promised his safe return home. A crayon portrait by Saint-Memin.

every time, just right. Firm with the Teton Sioux and the thieving Chinook. Friendly and generous with the many hospitable tribes who helped us."

Lewis interrupted. "Will Clark's describing himself," he said.

Captain McClallan laughed. "One thing I see. After two years together, you still admire each other. That says a lot."

The three friends talked until midnight. Learning that the expedition had very little food excepting the pawpaw fruit they had picked on the riverbank, McClallan gave his friends biscuits, chocolate, and sugar for the men.

"I can spare enough to last you the hundred and fifty miles downriver to St. Louis," he said.

While Clark and McClallan packed the food into the canoe, Lewis rested his healing leg against the boat's mast and thought of what Clark had said about handling the Indians. Maybe it wasn't too difficult, because we liked them, he thought.

We treated the Indians without fear, fairly and honestly as we would treat any man. I think they knew we were interested in their way of life and had not come to change it.

Three days later the men of the expedition shouted with joy when they saw the first sign of civilization, a herd of cows grazing along the riverbank.

It was Sunday afternoon when the boats reached St. Charles. Men, women, and children, strolling along the street, were startled by a salute of gunfire from the line of canoes. Oarsmen pulled faster and faster to reach the landing at the lower end of the town. The people who had waved the Corps good-by more than two years ago ran to meet them now, delighted and astonished to see the explorers. The men were invited to the homes of the citizens to eat and visit and sleep.

Early the next morning Lewis and Clark took Big White and his family to the public store, where the United States had a supply of Indian trading goods. They bought clothing of the chief's choice before taking him on to St. Louis to meet their friends. The captains continued to wear their buckskins until they could have clothes made by a tailor in St. Louis.

The people of St. Louis greeted the shouting, joyful men with surprise and delight. Old friends invited them into their homes and offered storerooms for their baggage. Everyone wanted to hear of the expedition's experiences during an absence of two years, four months, and ten days.

On the way downriver, Captain Lewis had written a long letter summarizing their adventures, so he could send it immediately to President Jefferson. Clark had copied it to send to his brother and his hometown newspaper in Kentucky.

Now, even before Lewis ate or changed clothes, he sent word to Postmaster John Hay to hold the postrider a few hours, long enough for Lewis to write Jefferson a covering note to tell him the Corps had reached St. Louis. If the mail moved at its usual rate over the seven hundred miles to Washington, President Jefferson should have the letter in twenty-seven days!

"September 23, 1806," Lewis began. "It is with pleasure that I announce to you the safe arrival of myself and my party at 12 o'clock noon today at this place with our papers and baggage. In obedience to your orders we have penetrated the continent of North America to the Pacific Ocean and sufficiently explored the interior of the country to affirm with confidence that we have discovered the most practical route which does exist across the continent, by means of the navigable branches of the Missouri and Columbia Rivers."

He praised his men who had stood up under the long journey with patience, courage, and fortitude. They were in good health and spirits, he wrote. He promised to bring the President's guest, Chief Big White, and family to Washington as soon as possible.

Captain Clark would remain in Kentucky with his family and the young woman he planned to marry.

Lewis wrote that he was anxious to see all his friends again. He particularly wanted to know if his mother was still living and well.

He ended his letter by saying: "With respect to the exertions and services rendered by that estimable man, Captain William Clark, in the course of the late voyage, I cannot say too much. If, sir, any credit be due for the success of that arduous enterprise in which we have been mutually engaged, he is equally with myself entitled to your consideration and that of our common country."

9
Governor of Upper Louisiana Territory

THE PEOPLE of St. Louis gave the first of many dinners in honor of the heroes of the expedition. When Lewis began the journey east with Big White, the party was entertained at every stop. At the towns along the rivers, there were banquets, speeches, and bonfires. Newspaper editors wrote that rivers should be named for Lewis and Clark. Poems were written about them. Their story spread throughout the states, as men recognized the great future for the United States that their exploration had made possible.

President Jefferson said, when Lewis finally reached him, "Your adventuring spirit has touched the hearts of all your countrymen and ensured your fame forever."

The first night in Washington, Captain Lewis took Big White and his party to the theater. They were accompanied by members of the Osage tribe and their agent, Pierre Chouteau, from northwest of St. Louis, who had also been invited to the capital. The Indians watched the show with delight and afterward entertained the audience with their tribal dances.

Following their initial introduction to Washington, Lewis left Chief Big White in the charge of Agent Chouteau, who would see that they enjoyed their visit. Lewis rode to Locust Hill to visit his family.

His mother held back tears as she embraced her "darling, affectionate, devoted son" again. He promised to send her a fine horse from a Spanish breed that he had admired very much in St. Louis.

He told his young half brother, John Marks, that he would pay the cost for John to attend medical lectures in Philadelphia. He would send the money as soon as he received his army pay, accumulated during his long absence.

Yes, he told his mother. He did hope to meet a girl to marry. So far his entire time and thought had been taken up by the expedition. He must still sort and rewrite the many notes he had stored in his pack trunks. When he had turned his notes and journals into a book, so the public could know the possibilities of the great West, he would settle down. Wherever he lived, he wanted his mother to come and live near him.

He stayed at Locust Hill only a few days. There was so much to do.

He wrote a long report of the expedition for Congress, so that it could compensate the men who had accompanied him.

He went to Philadelphia, where he discussed with the publisher, John Conrad, the cost of printing the book he planned to write. He went to the botanist, Frederick Pursh, with descriptions or specimens of dried plants he had brought home. Pursh said many species were unknown. Lewis paid him to examine and describe them scientifically for the book. Among the new species were two kinds of sagebrush, the buffalo berry, flowering currants, the Oregon grape, mountain holly, and evergreen huckleberry. Lewis described the immense size of the conifers of the West. A spruce he had measured was thirty-six feet around. The western hemlock and white pine rose to great height. A magnificent pine (Douglas) had thin bracts that protruded from among the cone scales.

He told Pursh of the beautiful wild flowers: mariposa lily, snow-on-the-mountain, scarlet mallow, and the blue camas. He said the camas flowers grew only in open flats where the soil was rich and moist and often under water. When the camas were in bloom, the prairie glades looked like lakes of blue water.

He engaged the famous painter, Charles Willson Peale, to illustrate some of the animals first seen by the explorers: grizzly bears, mountain goats, bighorn sheep, silver fox, marten, and prairie dogs. Peale was delighted with Lewis's visit, for he wanted to paint a portrait of the young explorer.

Lewis visited the ornithologist, Alexander Wilson, and asked him to classify and draw the new birds seen in the West, among them the magpie, the western white crane, and a large woodpecker with a rose-red breast, which Wilson named Lewis's woodpecker.

Clark was preparing maps for the book. Lewis himself would have to write it and arrange the detailed Indian vocabulary he had listed, a work of months, if not years.

On his return to Washington, Lewis spent many hours with Jefferson describing the value and the dangers of claiming the Far West. It was particularly important to send traders to the many tribes as Lewis had promised. He prepared a list of the items he had found most valuable in trading with the Indians and made a copy for Secretary of War Dearborn.

When he brought the list to the President, Lewis said, "I have just visited Chief Big White of the Mandans. He tells me that he has been royally entertained everywhere. He is convinced of the friendship and power of the Great Father of the United States. Now he wants to go home."

Jefferson told Lewis to see that the chief and his party got home. "I place you fully responsible for their safe return," Jefferson said. "You are authorized to take such measures as are necessary, and at the expense of the Government."

Lewis was detained in Washington when the Congress, on March 3, 1807, passed an act to compensate Captains Lewis and Clark and their men with grants of public land west of the Mississippi River. The two leaders received 1,600 acres each, their men 320 acres each. "It is only fair," the Congressmen agreed, "that such men receive a slight fraction of the vast territory which their dangerous adventure added to their country."

On the same day Congress approved President Jefferson's nomination of Captain Meriwether Lewis as Governor of the Territory of Upper Louisiana. A week later William Clark was named Superintendent of Indian Affairs in the same territory.

Lewis was overjoyed that he and Clark would continue to work together at St. Louis. He remained in Washington to complete work concerning the expedition and his book, but he sent Chief Big White to St. Louis with Pierre Chouteau. Lewis and Clark arranged for a trusted member of their expedition, Sergeant Pryor, to take Big White home.

Escorted by fourteen soldiers and twenty-two traders, the Big White party left St. Louis in boats on May 18, 1807. Later Pryor reported to Lewis what happened.

The Arikaras, who had been friendly to the expedition, fell upon Pryor's party and killed several of his men and wounded others. He had only saved Chief Big White and his family by turning back to St. Louis. Later he learned the reason for the Arikaras' anger. They had decided to send a chief to visit Washington. The chief died of pneumonia before he reached the city, but the Arikaras believed he had been killed there.

The mails were so slow that it was almost two months before Lewis learned that Big White and his family had failed to get past the Arikaras on the Missouri. Lewis wrote that he would attend to the matter as soon as he could leave Washington, where he was still detained by business for Jefferson and by writing his book.

Lewis reached St. Louis in March, 1808, to take over his duties as governor. Once again he made plans to return Big White to the Mandan village. Clark had not yet come from Kentucky with his bride, so Lewis discussed the situation with Frederick Bates, Secretary for Louisiana, who had been acting governor until Lewis arrived.

Secretary Bates said that Indian affairs had gone from bad to worse. English traders who wanted the rich fur trade on the Missouri had gone among the Indian tribes and turned them against the United States.

Governor Lewis knew that he dared not send Big White through hostile Indian country without a large armed escort. Yet he could not spare soldiers from the militia, for American ships were having trouble with English ships at sea. In case of a British attack up the Mississippi River, he would need the militia to defend the town.

Governor Lewis immediately began to repair relations with the Indians, for he saw that Bates had had little patience with them. Lewis sent traders to the tribes with the trade goods they prized. He also sent renewed messages of friendship from the Government of the United States. In June he was delighted to hear that the Superintendent of Indian Affairs, William Clark, was on his way to St. Louis with his bride.

Lewis met them at the landing and took Will and Judy Clark to the house he had found for them. For several days the three friends went together to welcoming dinners and parties given by the townspeople. They were well liked by the old French and Spanish settlers as well as the newer Americans.

Only Secretary Bates troubled the new governor. He scarcely

spoke to Lewis at social affairs and was difficult to deal with in business.

"I don't know why he dislikes me," Lewis said to Clark one night as they talked together before the fireplace in his friend's home. "You get along with him."

Clark laughed briefly. "He doesn't want my job," he said. "You were absent in Washington long enough for him to develop a taste for being governor."

Lewis, who had always been generous in praise of the men with whom he worked, changed the subject. He told his friend about some of the things he had been doing since he had reached St. Louis.

He had invited Jusseaume's thirteen-year-old French-Indian son to remain. Lewis was going to pay for his education. "He's a bright boy," he said.

Lewis said the first newspaper in the town would be published the next week. He had financed the *Missouri Gazette* from his own pocket, since he felt the town needed it.

And he was buying land, Lewis told his friend. He had invested all his cash, even borrowed money, to buy land. St. Louis was growing and had a great future. He had asked his mother to sell some of their Virginia land, then come here to live. Already he had taken an option on a thousand acres with a good house that he thought she and his family would like.

Then the two men got down to the real issue troubling them, Indian affairs. The Osages, with whom they had been negotiating a treaty, were plundering settlers again. Tribes along the Mississippi River, north, were threatening war. The Arikaras, after defeating Pryor's men with Chief Big White, had completely closed the Missouri River to travelers above their village.

"I believe in time we can win most of the hostile tribes again," Governor Lewis said, "but Big White must be returned to his people as soon as possible. We promised. The Government of the United States is humiliated until we keep that promise. It's a point of honor."

"It must be done," Clark agreed.

From that day on the two men worked together to show the Indian tribes that the United States intended to be their friends and expected them to keep their part of any bargain. Clark often went to visit and speak to the Indians.

He and Governor Lewis had seventy trusted scouts trained to go to the tribes with messages and with tools and other useful items promised to them. They sent invitations for chiefs to come to St. Louis for treaty talks. Gradually most of the nearby tribes were won to "Our Father Lewis."

Jefferson's term as President had ended, and James Madison was elected President before Governor Lewis finally thought it safe to send Big White back up the Missouri River to his home. The governor contracted with the St. Louis Missouri Fur Company, a large band of traders and trappers known to him, to escort the chief and his family. Lewis reinforced the Fur Company with 120 hired soldiers, armed with rifles and ammunition. Some of these men came from Daniel Boone's town, not far away, although Daniel Boone was past seventy years, too old to go.

Indian Agent Pierre Chouteau was in charge of the small army. Lewis told him that Congress had appropriated the sum of seven thousand dollars to pay the men to get Big White home. They would be paid if they delivered him safely. They would receive nothing if they failed.

Before Big White was to leave, Clark and Chouteau came to the governor with a new problem. Trusted scouts had informed them that the Arikaras had been joined by the powerful Cheyenne tribe. Both were determined not to let any boat pass beyond their territory on the Missouri. Their combined warriors numbered in the hundreds and were armed.

Clark and Chouteau suggested that Chouteau take an extra

supply of prize trading goods: tools, ammunition, and guns. Then, if he met heavy resistance, he could use the trading goods to hire additional warriors from friendly tribes on the Missouri.

Lewis was troubled. He did not believe in paying Indians not to aggress. He said bribery only encouraged the Indians to worse acts in hope of greater gains. Still, more trading goods to hire additional allies in case of a fight seemed necessary to ensure that Big White reached home.

More trading goods meant more money. It would take months to write to the war office in Washington, and receive a reply, for permission to spend extra money. The Fur Company could not wait, since they planned to go on up the Missouri for the winter when they had delivered the Mandan chief. Jefferson had ordered Lewis to do what he must do to return Big White, no matter what it cost.

Governor Lewis signed a voucher for the extra, expensive trade supplies. "If it is not necessary to use these, you will see that the United States receives full credit for them later," he instructed Chouteau. The Indian agent agreed.

In mid-May, 1809, more than a year after Lewis had taken up residence as governor, he told Chief Big White good-by as the Fur Company started up the Missouri River. Then Lewis returned to the many problems of governing the new territory.

On a hot, muggy July day, Governor Lewis received a letter from Washington in reply to his report on the Big White problem. He was pleased, for he had been expecting payment of the bills he had sent to the Secretary of War so that he could pay the creditors in St. Louis.

The governor did not know William Eustis, the new Secretary of War, who had replaced his old friend Dearborn when Madison became President. But Lewis had carefully explained in his reports his reason for spending an extra five hundred dollars on

A contemporary portrait of Meriwether Lewis, governor of the
Territory of Upper Louisiana, by Saint-Memin.

supplies for Big White's return. He had also explained other bills, such as having the U.S. laws of the territory translated into Spanish so the many Spanish-speaking citizens could read the laws.

When the governor opened the letter from Secretary Eustis, he could not have been more shocked if a bullet had exploded in his face. In sarcastic terms the new Secretary of War reminded Governor Lewis that his friend, Jefferson, was no longer President of the United States, and that Madison did not agree with Lewis's unauthorized spending of money.

"The Government of the United States," Eustis wrote, "should have been consulted before spending $500 for tobacco, powder, and trade goods for the Indians. We cannot honor the governor's bill for these goods, or bills for any other purpose for which the Government has not given prior approval."

Governor Lewis walked the floor of his office. Jefferson and Dearborn had understood the tangled, difficult job of governing a new territory of mixed nationalities—the old French and Spanish settlers, new settlers from the United States, the suspicious Indians who changed their minds often and warred among themselves. Jefferson and Dearborn had known that Lewis had to have power to act on his own. How could he make Madison and Eustis understand?

Not by writing, he decided. The letter he held in his hand was almost two months old. His creditors were expecting their money. Lewis had promised that he would pay the merchants as soon as he heard from Washington.

He sent his Spanish manservant, Pernia, to Clark and asked his friend to come to the office.

When Clark arrived, Lewis told him that he was going to Washington as soon as he could put the affairs of the government in order and attend to his personal business.

"For," he said to his friend, "I am personally responsible for these bills if the Government refuses to pay them. You know I am land poor. All I have is tied up in land. I shall be ruined if my creditors hear that the War Department refused the bills. Each one will come down on me quickly, hoping to get his money first. Even the Indians will be alarmed, thinking we cannot carry out our promises to them."

Clark said, "Secretary Eustis knows about as much about the problems of Louisiana Territory as a baby does. Write and ask Jefferson to talk to him."

"The mails are too slow," Lewis said. "Jefferson is at Monticello. He'd have to make a trip to Washington. Then I doubt that Eustis would listen, for he shows jealousy in his letter.

"No, I must go myself. Surely when I appear before the heads of the War and Treasury Departments and answer their questions, they cannot fail to see how necessary these bills are."

Lewis spent the next six weeks of the hot summer putting the governor's accounts in order so that Bates could administer them as acting governor. He turned over his personal accounts to Will Clark and two other friends to whom he gave his power of attorney.

"I leave a record of my debts and all my land as security," he told Clark. "If you are embarrassed by creditors in my absence, you must sell land and pay the bills."

He prepared for his journey to Washington as carefully as he had planned the expedition. Only this time there was no joy or anticipation. He was very tired as he packed his rifle, the famous air gun, which had impressed the Indians when he brought in so much game to feed them. It had been less exhausting to hunt on foot twenty miles in a day, he thought, than it was to cope with the jealousy, delay, and misunderstanding in government.

He was going by boat down the Mississippi to New Orleans,

where he would take passage on a ship by sea to Washington. He could take as much baggage as he wished. He filled four pack trunks. He took journals, notes, and many pages of the manuscript he had completed for his book. He packed good clothing, too, for he must live up to his position as governor when he called on the President and the Secretary of State. He stuffed a large portfolio with copies of the disputed bills and his letters of explanation.

Since Lewis would ride horseback after he left the ship, he asked Pernia to pack a bridle and his saddle trimmed with fine Spanish silver. In one of the pack trunks, Lewis placed his pipe tomahawk, and the dirk he had worn on the expedition. He carried two pistols made by one of the best gunsmiths. No man went on a long trip unarmed when there were hostile Indians along the river and plundering British ships at sea.

The governor asked Pernia to see that the trunks were placed safely on the boats. "Stay with them until I come aboard," he said. "They are of great value."

His Spanish servant gave him a quick, searching look. Pernia probably thinks the trunks are filled with gold, Lewis thought. He would scarcely believe that Lewis might value only papers and journals so highly. Still, Pernia was good with horses and had no family, so he was free to accompany Lewis on the trip.

On August 30, Lewis met with his council for last-minute instructions. He would go first to Washington, he said, then to see his mother, and return to St. Louis as soon as possible.

By the time the boat carrying Lewis and Pernia had moved down the Mississippi and stopped at Fort Pickering, Lewis was very ill. An old friend from army days, Captain Gilbert Russell, was in charge of the small force at Fort Pickering. He met the boat at the landing. When he saw Lewis was exhausted and shaking with fever, the captain took the governor to his quarters and called a surgeon's mate. Together they treated Lewis for malaria, which many persons had that hot humid summer.

The next morning Lewis was better but weak. He said to Captain Russell, "I hope I did not trouble you too much with my babbling last night. The fever always makes me lightheaded."

"You're still not well enough to travel," the Captain said. "Stay and rest until the next boat."

During breakfast Lewis told Russell the reasons for his trip to Washington to explain his bills. "I can't waste time," he said, "or my creditors may call in my notes and ruin me financially."

Captain Russell said that he, too, was having trouble with the new Administration, which had refused some of his vouchers for supplies for the fort.

"I've applied for leave to go to Washington and expect permission to leave the fort any day," Russell said. "I've decided to go overland, with an escort of several soldiers, take the Natchez Trace through Tennessee to Virginia. I decided against going by sea, too many ships have been taken below the port of New Orleans."

Lewis frowned. "I heard the pirate Lafitte was active," he said.

"Jean Lafitte won't capture a ship flying the American flag," Russell said. "British ships are the threat. The British have been boarding American vessels at sea and pressing our sailors into service on their ships."

Lewis thought fast. He was not so much concerned for himself. But the information he carried on the Far West, his journals and maps, must not fall into British hands. He could not afford the risk of going by sea.

"I've changed my mind," he said. "I'll go overland to Washington. Can you sell me two good horses and some pack animals on credit?"

"I'll do better than that," Captain Russell said. "We'll go together, if you'll wait a few days until my orders come through.

The Natchez Trace is dangerous. We'll both be safer in each other's company."

After ten days Captain Russell still had not received permission from Washington to leave the fort. Lewis told him that he must go on alone. He was anxious to get his work done.

Knowing the dangers of the long wilderness trip overland, Governor Lewis wrote a letter to President Madison: "Dear Sir: I arrived here very much exhausted from the heat of the climate, but having medicine feel better. My fear of the original papers relative to my voyage to the Pacific Ocean falling into the hands of the British induced me to change my route and proceed by land through the state of Tennessee to the City of Washington. I bring with me duplicates of my vouchers for public expenditures & which, when fully explained, or rather the general view of the circumstances under which they were made, I flatter myself they will receive both approbation and sanction. Providing my health permits, no time will be lost in reaching Washington."

Governor Lewis gave the letter to Captain Russell to be sent by postrider when the mail came through.

"Thieves rarely bother the postrider on the Natchez Trace," Russell said. "They're not interested in letters. But many men with pack trunks like yours have been murdered. They'd kill you for that silver-trimmed bridle and saddle on your horse. I wish you would wait for me."

"I must go," Lewis said.

"At least wait until morning," Russell urged. "James Neelly, the Indian agent for the Chickasaw nation, is taking some horses to Nashville. You could ride that far with him."

"I'll be pleased to have company," Lewis said. "Isn't Neelly the man I've seen with Pernia?"

"Neelly and your man, Pernia, have something in common," Captain Russell said drily. "The bottle. Still, Neelly knows the trail, and the Chickasaws aren't likely to bother you if he is along."

Lewis repacked his baggage. He took the most important papers in two pack trunks on horses. He left the other two trunks with Russell to send later. He also borrowed money from Russell, since he knew that his expenses along the way might be more than he had anticipated by ship.

On September 29, Governor Lewis began his journey overland on horseback, accompanied by Pernia, Agent Neelly, and Neelly's black servant, Tom. Several Chickasaw Indians rode with them as far as the Chickasaw agency not far from the Natchez Trace. Then the four men and their small herd of horses filed along the old Indian trail that ran northeast to the Tennessee River.

It's hardly a road, Lewis thought, as he passed under tall pines that met overhead and shut out the sun, even in daylight. Yet the Natchez Trail, whacked through the underbrush, was the only passage men had from the settlements on the Atlantic Coast into the West and South. It was worn deep by travel like the buffalo trails Lewis had seen on the western prairie.

At night the men camped beside the Trace, where swamp water had killed a few trees. In the cool gloom mists rose as the wet soil cooled.

Lewis built a very small fire, a trick he had learned from the Indians. A big fire burned a man's face and let his back get cold, the Nez Percés had told him. A man can get close to a little fire and keep warm all over.

When they had eaten, Neelly brought out a bottle and began to talk.

"Mighty few taverns along the Trace," he said, "and what there is shouldn't rightly be called taverns—not like those in your state of Virginia, Governor. On the Trace, there's just cabins with a tavern sign dangling outside. Maybe one room for guests. Everybody got to sleep together. They'll give you a meal and some corn whiskey and a lot of talk, usually.

"If that's all a man had to watch out for, it wouldn't be too bad. But last year sheriff caught a tavern keeper that had too many guests disappear. Seems like this feller was a real good host, treated guests handsomely until he took them to their beds and blew out the candles. When they was snoring real good, the host slipped back to the cabin, and pushed the door open slowly. But he moved like a cat, with a hand swift as lightning with steel in it.

"It was a long time before the law caught him, because he only took the guests' purses. He run their horses off into the wilderness, burned all their clothing, and cut up the bridles and buried them."

Lewis spread his buffalo robe on the ground, avoiding the gnarled roots of trees that crawled along the high bank.

Neely looked across the bed of coals and said, "Be safer, Governor, if you was to dig a hole under your robe and bury that pouch of money you're carrying. Be easy for some Trace pirate to lift it off you while you sleep."

Lewis touched the dirk he wore in his belt to see that it was loose. He placed his two pistols beside him.

"Thank you," he said. "I'm a light sleeper."

After more than a week on the road, the travelers crossed the Tennessee River and camped at Dogwood Mudhole on the ninth of October. The next morning Neely told Lewis that two of his horses had broken away in the night and strayed. He would have to stay and hunt them. He sent his black servant, Tom, with Lewis and Pernia.

"Wait for me at the next tavern you come to," he said. "Grinder's Stand is about a day's ride, at Little Swan Creek."

Toward evening Governor Lewis, riding ahead of Pernia and Tom, who were herding the extra horses, came out of the canopy of trees into a clearing. Two small log cabins faced the Trace, joined by a hallway about twelve feet long. A crudely lettered sign hung above a door, GRINDER'S STAND.

Lewis entered the cabin. A middle-aged woman in a homespun dress turned from the fireplace.

Lewis introduced himself and asked for food and lodging for the night. She said she was Mrs. Robert Grinder. Her husband was not at home. One of the governor's own men would have to take the horse to the stable.

Surely, she added, such an elegant man was not riding the Trace without an escort?

Courteously Lewis said that two menservants were just behind him with horses, and that Agent Neelly would arrive later to stay overnight.

The woman showed Governor Lewis the one-room guest cabin, with doors made of split oak on wooden hinges. He unsaddled his horse and carried the saddle into the room, along with his packet of important bills and records for the War Department. Then he looked around.

The openings between the logs in the walls were unusually wide, as much as four inches. The cracks had been filled with wood chips daubed with clay. Many chips were loose and could be lifted out at will, an easy entry for a rifle barrel.

Pernia and Tom came up with the horses. Pernia brought in the pack trunks and placed them in the room. Lewis asked him to sleep in the stable and keep an eye on the horses. A robe spread on clean straw there would be every bit as inviting as this cabin.

When Mrs. Grinder called him to supper, Lewis ate very little. He had never felt as alone on the prairie as he did at this table in the half-dark cabin. He wished Will Clark were sitting across from him. They always had plenty to say to each other.

He went to the open door and looked up at a line of birds flying across the reddening sky. "What a sweet evening this is," he said.

He walked a little way up the Trace to a knoll where he could see the sunset. A mockingbird called. He thought of the pet mockingbird that used to ride on Jefferson's shoulder. It would be good to go to Monticello and see his older friend again.

He liked the smell of damp fallen leaves mixed with the fragrance of tall pine. The oaks and dogwood were turning gold and deep red. And there was a cluster of wild purple asters like those he used to pick for his mother when he was a boy. A while ago, he thought, for he had turned thirty-five years old a few weeks earlier.

He picked an aster and saw that its fragile petals had already folded up for the night. Wild asters were not a good cut flower, but his mother had always arranged them in a dish on the table when he brought them to her.

How good it would be to see her again.

He walked back along the Trace. There was no sign yet of Neelly with the lost horses. Lewis decided to go to bed early. It was perhaps seventy miles on to Nashville, and a week's ride more to Virginia. He wanted to be on the road again at daylight.

But the next morning, October 11, 1809, Governor Meriwether Lewis was dead, with a furrow across his forehead from a pistol shot. A second shot had gone through his body leaving a wound in his chest and another low near his backbone.

10
How Did He Die?

PROBABLY NO ONE will ever know how Lewis died. Of the persons *known* to be at Grinder's Stand that night, only Mrs. Grinder claimed to have witnessed his death. And over the course of a few years, she told several such different stories that historians cannot believe any one of them to be the truth.

Mrs. Grinder's first account was repeated by Agent Neelly in a letter he wrote from Nashville a week after Lewis died. He wrote to Jefferson saying that Governor Lewis had had a recurrence of the fever on the trail, that he had become lightheaded and irrational. And that Lewis had killed himself during the night at Grinder's Stand.

Neelly said that he was not there when it happened. He had not come up with the lost horses until the next morning.

Mrs. Grinder had met Neelly and told him that she was awakened by the sound of a gun in the guest cabin at three o'clock in the morning. She had heard a thud as if a man fell to the floor, and the words, "Oh, Lord." There was another pistol shot. Several minutes later Lewis called out and asked for water. But, she said, she had been *alone* in the house and so terrified that she had not gone to his room.

Scene of Lewis's last, ill-fated journey, the Natchez Trace, as it now looks near Duck River Ridge, Tennessee. Two-century-old ruts still groove the path.

At sunrise she had gone to the stable and wakened Pernia, who went with her to the guest cabin. Lewis, barely alive, was reported to have said, "I have done the business, my good servant, give me water."

Neelly's letter continued: "She said he survived but a short time. I came up some time after and had him as decently buried as I could in that place.

"I have got in my possession his two trunks of papers (amongst which is said to be his travels to the Pacific Ocean) and probably some vouchers for a bill which he said had been protested by the Secretary of War.

"I have also in my care his rifle, silver watch, brace of pistols, dirk, and tomahawk. One of the Governor's horses was lost in the wilderness which I will endeavor to regain, and the other I have sent on by his servant [Pernia] who expressed a desire to go to the Governor's mother and to Monticello. I have furnished him with fifteen dollars to defray his expenses to them. I wish to be informed what arrangements may be considered best in sending on his trunks. [Signed] James Neelly, U.S. Agent to the Chickasaw Nation."

Thomas Jefferson received Neelly's letter at Monticello six weeks after Lewis's death. Having no details concerning the governor's wounds, the shocked and grieving Jefferson accepted the flat statement that Lewis killed himself. He made no investigation, possibly to spare the good name of such a man from the crime of suicide.

At that time Jefferson could not know that Neelly took all of Lewis's valuable private property, except the trunks. (Two years later young John Marks went to see his half brother's grave. Then he rode on to Neelly's home. Mrs. Neelly said that her husband was away, and he always wore Lewis's pistols and dirk. She gave up Lewis's horse and rifle.)

At first, William Clark, too, accepted the report that Lewis had died by his own hand. Clark came to Nashville to take charge of his friend's trunks of papers, since he had Lewis's power of attorney. Again, due to the slow travel of those days, Lewis had been dead for some months when Clark reached Nashville. He found that the people of Tennessee were telling many different stories about the death of the young governor.

Lewis had been murdered, people said. The pouch of money he carried, containing at least $120, according to Captain Russell, was never found. Russell had also said that Neelly had no money on him when he left Fort Pickering with Lewis. How, then, had Neelly given fifteen dollars to Pernia to go to Locust Hill?

People asked: Had Neelly really lost two horses along the Trace? Or had he made this excuse to remain behind as an alibi, then slipped into Grinder's cabin at night to rob Lewis?

Had Pernia been in on the plan? Had Neelly paid for Pernia's silence with his own employer's money?

Pernia had gone to Mrs. Lucy Marks and told her that her son shot himself. Pernia asked her to pay him the back wages that Lewis owed him, a sum of $240, he said.

Lucy Marks questioned Pernia closely. She insisted on knowing every detail, for, she said, her son would not kill himself. He had written her how much he was looking forward to coming home. He was always optimistic, a fighter. If he failed to overcome an obstacle in one way, he would try another. The Government's mistake about the bill would never have driven him to this end.

"Did Mrs. Grinder *see* Lewis kill himself?" she asked.

"No," Pernia admitted. "She heard the shots."

Pernia must have described the wounds and Mrs. Grinder's claim that Lewis did not die for four hours.

Then, people said, Lucy Marks really turned upon Pernia with

A reconstruction of Grinder's Inn, now in a public park in Tennessee. The original site of Lewis's death burned soon afterward, with critical evidence.

scorn and anger. Did he expect her to believe that her son would make such a botch of shooting himself, if he had done such a thing? Meriwether Lewis was a perfect shot even as a boy. If he had killed himself, he would have done the job with one quick shot.

She accused Pernia of having robbed and killed his master. Pernia was riding Lewis's horse and wearing Lewis's clothing. Now he hoped to get money from the family through a claim of back wages!

Clark, too, hearing of the two awkward shots from which Lewis had died, agreed that Lewis would have killed himself neatly, and at once, if he had done it.

Clark heard other stories repeated in the Nashville area. The man, Grinder, had been working only a short distance from home. Had he returned in the night, heard from his wife about the famous man, with valuable trunks and money, who was asleep in the guest cabin? Grinder could have slipped in to steal, people said. Lewis waked and tried to protect his valuables. In the ensuing fight, Grinder shot him twice. Finding such a famous guest dying in the tavern, the Grinders had made up the story of suicide, Grinder then went away. Mrs. Grinder called Pernia only after Lewis was too weak to tell the true story.

Other persons said that Grinder was known to sell whiskey to the Indians, although this was against the law. Often Indians came at night to buy whiskey. Moccasin tracks had been found near the Grinder's corn crib, and the print of a rifle butt, a print peculiar to the rifle owned by a half-breed bandit known as Runnions. Had the bandit, hidden in the trees along the Trace, watched Lewis stop at Grinder's Stand, and come later to rob him?

Clark heard an even more startling story. A postrider carrying mail, Robert Smith, said he had passed Grinder's Stand about ten o'clock on October 11. He found the body of Governor Lewis beside the Trace, Lewis had fallen forward as if he had sat down and braced himself against the trunk of a tree. It appeared from marks in the road that he had crawled there from the cabin, a distance of about 150 yards. Later Smith had searched the ground and found the wadding from a musket between the dead man and the stable.

Here was certainly a riddle. How could Lewis have died on his bed in the cabin with Mrs. Grinder and Pernia looking on, as Mrs. Grinder first reported, then crawled to the Trace and propped himself against a tree to die? It was more likely that his assassin had shot him in the cabin, and Lewis tried to escape by crawling to the Trace in the dark after Mrs. Grinder refused to come to his aid.

At a later date Mrs. Grinder changed her story to fit that of the postrider's. She said she had *not* been *alone* in the house the night Lewis died. She had witnesses. Her half-grown son and daughter had been with her. After they heard the shots, they had opened the chink in the cabin walls and seen Lewis crawl across the yard to the Trace, probably after water from a small brook beyond. Terrified, she had waited until morning, then *sent her children* to the stable after Pernia.

Which was true? Was she alone that night? Did she go herself to the stable after Pernia at daybreak, when the two of them stood beside Lewis's bed as he died, as she first stated? Or was her second story correct? She told a third revised version two years later to the ornithologist, Wilson, when he visited Lewis's grave.

Now a man from the Grinder neighborhood made a statement that fully convinced Clark, and many others, that Governor Lewis was murdered. The neighbor said that Agent Neelly had hired a Mr. Cooper, a blacksmith living about fifteen miles from the Grinders, to make a split-oak box in which to bury Lewis. The neighbor had helped place the Governor in the box. He said

The only monument to Meriwether Lewis was built many years after his death by the State of Tennessee, a broken column near the site of Grinder's cabins.

the shots that killed Lewis had gone *in* his back and come *out* his chest, the opposite of the story told by the Grinders.

With all this conflicting evidence, the authorities in Tennessee felt unable to arrest and convict anyone.

The Government of the United States never made an official investigation. Possibly President Madison was trying to follow Jefferson's wish to spare Lewis's good name and his family. Possibly the Government was embarrassed by its part in bringing Lewis on the fatal journey.

The people of St. Louis, far from the scene of their Governor's death, heard the news with sorrow. Few believed that he had committed suicide. One of the officials of the Upper Louisiana Territory said, "Young Governor Lewis was well liked, a brave, honorable, honest, fair man. Of excellent judgment, he was respected by the inhabitants, French, Spanish, Americans, and Indians alike. Nothing in his actions ever indicated that he would do an act so extraordinary and unexpected."

All that historians know is that anything could have happened after Lewis entered Grinder's cabin that night. No reliable witness stated the facts.

Although Lewis never reached Washington, his letters to President Madison and his carefully kept records and bills were sent to Congress. In March, 1812, the War Department agreed that Lewis had done only what he was required to do under Jefferson's original order, returned Big White to his tribe safely. The disputed bills were allowed. The money was paid to Lewis's estate.

The only monument to Meriwether Lewis is one built many years after his death by the State of Tennessee. It is a broken column near the grave of the great pathfinder in a small national park that includes a length of the Natchez Trace and the site of Grinder's cabins.

MERIWETHER LEWIS
1774–1809,

BENEATH THIS MONUMENT ERECTED UNDER LEGISLATIVE ACT BY THE STATE OF TENNESSEE, A.D. 1848, REPOSES THE DUST OF MERIWETHER LEWIS, A CAPTAIN IN THE UNITED STATES ARMY, PRIVATE SECRETARY TO PRESIDENT JEFFERSON, SENIOR COMMANDER OF THE LEWIS AND CLARK EXPEDITION, AND GOVERNOR OF THE TERRITORY OF LOUISIANA.

IN THE GRINDER HOUSE, THE RUINS OF WHICH ARE STILL DISCERNIBLE, 230 YARDS SOUTH OF THIS SPOT, HIS LIFE OF ROMANTIC ENDEAVOR AND LASTING ACHIEVEMENT CAME TRAGICALLY AND MYSTERIOUSLY TO ITS CLOSE ON THE NIGHT OF OCT. 11, 1809.

THE REPORT OF THE COMMITTEE APPOINTED TO CARRY OUT THE PROVISIONS OF THE MONUMENT ACT, CONTAINS THESE SIGNIFICANT STATEMENTS: "GREAT CARE WAS TAKEN TO IDENTIFY THE GRAVE. GEORGE NIXON, ESQ., ... ACQUAINTED WITH THE LOCALITY. ... AN OLD SURVEYOR, HAD BECOME VERY EARLY ... HE POINTED OUT THE PLACE, BUT TO MAKE ASSURANCE DOUBLY SURE, THE GRAVE WAS RE-OPENED AND THE UPPER PORTION OF THE SKELETON EXAMINED AND SUCH EVIDENCE FOUND AS TO LEAVE NO DOUBT OF THE PLACE OF INTERMENT."

The sign tells of difficulty in locating the unmarked, hastily dug grave.

His real monument is in the hearts of those who recognize what he did for America. Among them are Elliott Coues, who wrote: "The story of his adventure stands easily first and alone. It is our national epic of exploration." Historian Hiram Chittenden calls Lewis's expedition, "Incomparably the most perfect achievement of its kind in the history of the world." To Vardis Fisher, Meriwether Lewis is "the greatest American of his breed and the most neglected."

Jefferson had a grand dream: an America wide and free from sea to sea. Lewis made the dream come true!

For Further Reading

THE AUTHOR is indebted to the following writers and recommends them to readers who want to know more about the great pathfinder:

Bakeless, John, *Lewis and Clark, Partners in Discovery.* William Morrow & Company, Inc., 1947.

DeVoto, Bernard, ed., *The Journals of Lewis and Clark.* Houghton Mifflin Company, 1953.

Dillon, Richard, *Meriwether Lewis: A Biography.* Coward-McCann, Inc., 1965.

Fisher, Vardis, *Suicide or Murder? The Strange Death of Governor Meriwether Lewis.* Alan Swallow, 1962.

About the Author

WILMA PITCHFORD HAYS has written thirty-seven books, fiction and nonfiction for children of all ages, many with authentic historical backgrounds. Born in Nebraska, she began at an early age to "make up" stories for her younger brother and four sisters. Later she told stories to her daughter and now tells them to her three grandchildren.

Mrs. Hays has worked with children all her life. She was a teacher before she married a superintendent of schools. Their daughter became a supervisor of music in public schools. When she sang in the musical *The Sound of Music,* she helped to coach the children in that show during a year's tour across the United States.

Mrs. Hays says, "I began writing for adults, but found children such wonderfully appreciative readers that I continued writing for them after publication of my first children's book *Pilgrim Thanksgiving,* in 1955."

The author enjoys summer in New England but returns to her home in Venice, Florida, during the winter, where she writes and also enjoys walking on the Gulf beaches to pick up shells and fossils.

Index